The Culinary Chronicles a Journey through Food and Cooking

Zara Khan

Author: Zara Khan

Title: The Culinary Chronicles a Journey through Food and Cooking

This book was printed and published by in [2023].

ISBN:

Table of Content

Chapter 1.
Travels for Epicureans:

Travel to various corners of the world, exploring regional cuisines, culinary traditions, and the stories behind iconic dishes.

Adventures in Food Travel: Tasting Your Way Around the World and Learning the History of Famous Dishes and Their Ingredients

The world is a rich patchwork of civilizations, each with its own distinct set of norms, practices, and lexicon. The common language of food provides a compelling window into this varied culture. It is a journey that transcends borders and overcomes gaps, allowing us to study the core of a culture, its history, and the stories of its people. We set out on a gourmet adventure in "The Culinary Chronicles: A Journey Through Food and Cooking," visiting far-flung locales to learn about local fare, age-old cooking practices, and the history behind some of the world's most recognizable meals.

The Complex Web of Flavors Weaved

Exploring new cuisines is like setting out on an exciting journey, with each dish representing a thrilling new chapter in a novel of tastes. Bangkok's hectic streets and Tuscany's bucolic countryside both provide very different dining experiences.

The streets of Thailand are lined with vendors selling all kinds of colorful and fragrant street cuisine. Tom Yum soup's savory and spicy notes, green curry's velvety smoothness, and mango sticky rice's sweet pleasure all tell the tale of a society that relishes in robust and contrasting flavors. As we take our time savoring each bite, we learn more about Thai cooking and its use of fresh herbs, nuanced spice combinations, and careful attention to flavor balance.

When we go across the world to Italy, we arrive in the center of the Mediterranean, amidst rolling vineyards and old olive groves. In this article, we delve into the sophistication and ease of Italian cooking, a style that places a premium on using fresh, natural ingredients. Each taste tells the tale of a country that cherishes history, family, and the joys of the table, from the silky smoothness of homemade pasta to the aromatic appeal of fresh basil and tomatoes in a Caprese salad.

Traditional Cooking: A Master Class

The fabric of any society is woven with the threads of its culinary traditions. The fact that they continue to be passed down from one generation to the next is a powerful symbol of the continuity between the past and the present.

Making sushi is a sacred craft in Japan that has been practiced for millennia. The commitment to excellence shines through in every detail, from the clean cuts of sashimi to the artful construction of a sushi roll. Sushi is more than simply food; it embodies the values of simplicity, minimalism, and craftsmanship that are important to Japanese society.

Making tortillas by hand is emblematic of Mexico's cultural history. Masa, or maize dough, is rolled out, flattened, and cooked on a griddle; it's then stuffed with a variety of delicious ingredients. The ancient Maya and Aztec civilizations left an unmistakable imprint on Mexican food, and you can taste it in every tortilla.

Famous Food: History Served Up on a Plate

Every civilization has its signature dishes that have come to represent that civilization around the world. These meals typically have stories attached to them that go beyond the world of flavor.
In India, the curry scent entices us, and we follow it to the famed Chicken Tikka Masala. Legend has it that a diner in the busy streets of

Glasgow, Scotland, asked for a gravy to go with their dry tandoori chicken, and thus this creamy and spicy dish was formed. This meal, which combines Indian spices with British techniques, is a perfect example of how cuisines can and do change over time.

The basic yet iconic hot dog has a history that transcends continents, from the street sellers of New York City to the quaint bistros of Paris. This humble but delicious treat has become an emblem of the fast food industry. It's convenient, sure, but it also serves as a reminder of the many cultures that have contributed to American food.

The Pleasures of Trying New Foods

Discovering new flavors is only part of the fun of trying dishes from other regions. It's the excitement of discovering a delicious new restaurant in a crowded metropolis, or the allure of browsing a local market stocked with colorful fruits, vegetables, and spices.

On our travels through Morocco, we learn about the wonderful world of tagine cooking. Like the clay pot it's cooked in, the tales of the nomadic Berbers and the exotic spices of North Africa are embedded in this hearty stew. Friends and family gather around the community pot to enjoy the dish's aromatic bounty, making it a dish that exemplifies the spirit of sharing.

New Orleans' food reflects the city's multicultural population and location in the heart of the American South. The gumbo is a fusion of French, Spanish, and African cuisines that results in a hearty and flavorful stew. The meal reflects the city's multicultural past, with ingredients and techniques borrowed from many different cultures.

Connecting Through Food and Story

In the end, it's not just about the food when it comes to learning about and appreciating other cultures' culinary traditions. It's the friendly greetings from the local cooks, the interesting discussions with other diners, and the mutual respect for the culinary arts.

When we sit down to a bowl of Pho in Vietnam, we are welcomed into a world of community. Vietnamese people's strength and solidarity can be tasted in this aromatic noodle soup made with fresh herbs, tender pork, and chewy rice noodles. Every slurp is a celebration of the Vietnamese people and their resilience, as its origins are tied to the country's ups and downs.

Meze, the Greek custom of sharing small meals and discussion with friends, is a source of great pleasure for visitors to Greece. Olives, feta cheese, tzatziki, and grilled octopus fill the table. The food tastes great, the wine flows freely, and everyone has a great time. To eat meze is to celebrate life itself; it's more than just a meal.

An Infinite Quest

Exploring new cuisines is an adventure with no final destination. It's an endless journey with fresh stops, strange people, and changing preferences. The more places we visit, the more we realize how much the same universal language of food unites people of all backgrounds and origins.

The book "The Culinary Chronicles: A Journey Through Food and Cooking" is a call to adventure. It's a passport to the world's kitchens, a guide to comprehending the stories spoken via flavors, and a celebration of the shared human experience that is the joy of eating. No matter how much you've seen or traveled, there's always more to learn, and the world's gastronomic treasures are just waiting to be discovered. Happy eating!

Chapter 2.
Time travel for your taste buds:

Take a historical journey through the evolution of food and cooking techniques, from ancient culinary practices to modern gastronomy.

Exploring the Past, Present, and Future of Food and Cooking

Food is fundamental to human life; it's a requirement that has developed into an art form, a vehicle for cultural expression, and a wellspring of creative ideas. The history of cuisine and culinary methods is a fascinating window into the past, present, and future of humankind. In this investigation, we will travel through time, following the path of food and cookery from its earliest days to the cutting edge of contemporary cuisine.

The Beginning of Cooking's Creative Era

Our culinary adventure begins in antiquity, when our forebears had to figure out how to feed themselves with the limited resources at their disposal. Early humans were largely hunters and gatherers, reliant on raw ingredients for nutrition. However, as they learned to thrive in different settings and harness the power of fire, their culinary abilities developed.

The invention of the open flame for cooking was a watershed moment in our species' development. By adding heat, basic materials were changed into something more appealing, safer, and more easily digested. This game-changing development cleared the path for exciting new culinary developments and expanded human palates.

Traditional Methods of Ancient Cooking

Culinary traditions developed become an important feature of ancient societies. Geographical and climatic differences, resource availability, and cultural norms all had a role in shaping the distinctive culinary traditions of different cultures.

Agriculture in ancient Egypt relied heavily on the Nile River. The Egyptians were masters of agriculture and the kitchen, growing their own grains, fruits, and vegetables and making their own beer and bread. Their mythology reflected the importance of bread in their diet, with Osiris being dubbed the "Lord of Bread."

The ancient Greeks, meantime, lauded the skill of hosting symposia, or large social events where gastronomy, vino, and deep conversation were intermingled. Their skill in the kitchen inspired elaborate recipes, and their devotion to olive oil, cheese, and wine paved the way for the development of Mediterranean cuisine.

The Romans, famous for their lavish banquets, forever changed the way people eat. They perfected the science of flavor pairing by liberally dousing their food in herbs and spices. Apicius, author of the Roman cookbook "De re Coquinaria," recorded a number of dishes that exemplified the culture's high level of culinary expertise.

The widespread adoption of Roman cooking methods like braising and roasting had a significant impact on subsequent cuisines. The enormous road system of the Roman Empire facilitated the sharing of materials, recipes, and cooking methods from diverse regions, ultimately leading to a gastronomic melting pot.

A Flavorful Tapestry from the Middle Ages

Throughout Europe in the Middle Ages, a diverse array of culinary traditions flourished. The nobility enjoyed lavish feasts while the poor people survived on meager fare; this demonstrated the close connection between food and the feudal regime.

The use of spices, which had made their way to Europe from the East via trade channels, was a defining characteristic of medieval cooking.

Spices such as pepper, cinnamon, and nutmeg were highly appreciated, and they gave depth and complexity to recipes. The European spice trade was ignited by the perception that the use of spices was a mark of social status and refinement.

The development of the Middle Ages coincided with an improvement in cooking methods. The wealthy preferred to use spit roasting, which resulted in juicy meats, while the working class cooked their food in the more affordable methods of boiling and baking. The first significant milestone in the history of pastry and baking was the introduction of savory and sweet fillings for pies.

The Age of Great Cooking

The European Renaissance ushered in a golden age of refined cuisine, travel, and scholarship. A culinary renaissance was spurred by the sharing of recipes, ingredients, and cooking methods across geographical regions.

The fresh ingredients and straightforward preparation of Italian cuisine rose to prominence. Pasta cooked to a perfect al dente texture, flavorful sauces, and mastering the risotto became cornerstones of Italian cuisine. The New World discovery tomato arrived in Italy around this period, changing the face of pasta meals forever.

Modern cooking skills owe a great deal to France, as well. Grand dinners, complete with elaborate food sculptures and lavish displays, became popular during the Renaissance. Classical French cuisine and the use of base sauces like béchamel and velouté are typically linked to the French chef François Pierre La Varenne.

The Origins of Contemporary Cuisine

The 18th century was a watershed in the development of cooking methods. Georges Auguste Escoffier, a French chef, introduced the brigade system and emphasized precision and discipline in professional kitchens. His book, "Le Guide Culinaire," set the groundwork for modern gastronomy.

The methods and structure that Escoffier advocated for in the professional kitchen are being used today. He brought French cuisine to its zenith by emphasizing the five "mother sauces" and mastering the art of presentation.

What It's Like in the Modern Food Scene

The evolution of cooking methods accelerated over the twentieth and twenty-first centuries. Sous-vide cooking, molecular gastronomy, and high-tech appliances have all emerged as a result of technological advancements in the kitchen. The scope of possible culinary accomplishments has been widened as a result of these innovations.

Culinary traditions from all around the world have been blending thanks to globalization to produce new and intriguing dishes that can be found in cities all over the globe. The barriers between different cultures and their cuisines no longer exist. It's an international phenomenon in which chefs from all over the world fuse elements of other cuisines to make innovative new meals.

Food in the Future

There appears to be no end in sight to the development of new foods and cooking methods. An increasing focus on farm-to-table sourcing and cutting down on food waste is highlighting the need of ethical and sustainable methods. Our conception of food is changing as we investigate new ways to obtain protein, including from plants and laboratory-grown sources.

Innovation is constantly being pushed forward by developments in technology and culinary science. The way we cook and eat is evolving as a result of technological advances such as 3D food printing, precision cooking tools, and smart kitchen gadgets.

The idea of food as art is also gaining traction in the culinary world. In an effort to challenge our senses and preconceptions, experimental and avant-garde chefs are expanding the boundaries of classic cuisine.

The Never-Ending Quest for Flavor

The journey through the evolution of food and cooking techniques is a monument to the inventiveness and flexibility of the human spirit. We have a rich culinary tradition that spans the ages and reflects the many cultures that have contributed to shaping our modern world.

The book "The Culinary Chronicles: A Journey Through Food and Cooking" will take you on an incredible adventure through time and space as it follows the evolution of cooking methods from the very beginning of humanity to the present day. This is a tale of perseverance, creativity, and the everlasting bond that humans share with their food. The culinary journey never ends, whether you're a seasoned chef or an eager home cook, and there are always new things to learn and do. Happy eating!

Chapter 3.
Food Preparation Tools:

Delve into the fundamentals of cooking, covering everything from knife skills and essential cooking techniques to mastering the art of seasoning.

Learning the Ropes of the Kitchen, Knife Skills, and Beyond

The act of preparing food is more than just a means to an end; it's also a creative outlet, a science, and a personal journey. Cooking is an art form that, like any other, requires practice and mastery of the basics. Learn the fundamentals of cooking, from how to use a knife properly to how to properly season food, as we dig into the world of culinary arts. This is your culinary primer, a guide to unlocking your potential in the kitchen, and the gateway to a world of creativity and gastronomic delight.

Knife Skills: The Pulse of the Kitchen

Knife skills are the foundation of any successful chef's career. The knife is more than simply a kitchen implement; it's a chef's trusty right hand, a precision instrument that can make or break any dish. Acquiring expert knife skills has many benefits in the kitchen, including improved efficiency, improved presentation, and improved flavor.

We start off by learning about the components of a chef's knife and their functions. Learning the proper way to wield a knife, from its razor-sharp blade to its sturdy bolster and comfortable handle, is the first step toward becoming a skilled cook.

We stress the significance of learning how to properly handle knives in order to avoid injuries while cooking. This entails not just how to hold the knife, but also the claw grip and safe methods of slicing and chopping.

Knife care and upkeep are also important facets of knife expertise. Maintaining a knife's edge through frequent sharpening and honing keeps it performing at peak efficiency, and safe storage safeguards both the blade and the chef. A chef's best companion is a sharp, well-maintained knife.

Essential Skills for the Kitchen

Now that we have a firm grasp on how to use a knife, we can move on to the other fundamental cooking techniques that will serve as the cornerstones of our future success in the kitchen. Using these methods, you may turn ordinary foods into culinary masterpieces with a symphony of tastes.

Sautéing is a method of cooking in which little bits of food are cooked rapidly in a small amount of oil or butter over high heat. Even cooking and taste retention are achieved by using high heat and regular stirring.

roasting is a dry-heat cooking method that utilizes a very hot oven to prepare food. The ingredients' natural flavors are amplified while a caramelized surface and delicate inside are produced.

Third, grilling, which gives food a smokey flavor and distinctive grill markings. Meat, veggies, and even fruits all benefit from this cooking process. To master the art of grilling, it is essential to learn how to regulate the heat and employ marinades.

The and methods are boiling and blanching, respectively. Boiling is for fully cooking food, while blanching momentarily immerses food in boiling water before cooling it quickly to maintain color and texture, making it great for vegetables.

Braising: Braising combines two cooking techniques into one: first, food is seared in fat, and then it is slowly simmered in a liquid that imparts flavor. This method turns tough chunks of beef into a tender, flavorful meal.

Steaming is a low-heat cooking method that uses the steam produced by boiling water to gently prepare food. It's a healthy and flexible choice because the nutrients and flavors of the foods are preserved.

Frying, number seven, involves dipping food into heated oil and letting it sit there until it cooks on the inside and gets a crispy outside. Both shallow and deep frying necessitate the ability to precisely control the oil temperature.

How to Season Anything to Perfection

Seasoning is the finishing touch that takes a food from bland to delicious. It's the little touch that unlocks the full potential of your ingredients and sets your dishes apart. Any good cook needs to know how to properly use salt, pepper, herbs, spices, and other seasonings.

The most basic seasoning is salt, which brings out the innate flavors of food. Understanding the many forms of salt and learning how to season with them efficiently are essential skills for any cook.

Pepper is a great way to give food more flavor and complexity. Knowing the differences between black, white, and pink peppercorns and becoming an expert user of freshly ground pepper will take your seasoning skills to the next level.

Herbs, both fresh and dried, are a great way to give your food a unique flavor and a burst of vitality. We savor the aromas and tastes of basil, oregano, rosemary, and more as we discover how they complement different dishes.

Spices from different parts of the world give your dishes their own distinct flavors. The unique qualities of spices like cinnamon, cumin, coriander, and paprika are discussed, as well as their culinary applications.

And final taste is called umami and it has a savory, meaty taste. A deeper level of flavor can be achieved in cooking by learning about umami and incorporating items like soy sauce, mushrooms, and Parmesan cheese.

Citrus, vinegar, and fermented foods are all examples of acidic elements that help brighten and balance flavors. Adding just the right amount of acid to your foods can give them additional flavor and appeal.

Seasoning: It's All in the Science

It's impossible to separate the art of seasoning from the science of flavor. One of the secrets to perfect seasoning is learning how our taste buds and brains register flavor. The four basic flavors of sweet, sour, salty, and bitter are examined through the lens of theories like the flavor triangle.

Aroma plays a crucial part in how we interpret flavors. Garlic, onions, and herbs are all examples of aromatics that can be used in cooking to enhance flavor and produce a more nuanced sensory experience.

Advanced Techniques for Making Your Dishes Stand Out

You now have the tools you need to make a broad variety of foods, thanks to your proficiency with knives, the fundamentals of cooking, and the science of seasoning. However, true culinary expertise requires going beyond these foundational skills and infusing them with your individual flair and enthusiasm. The best chefs are the ones who aren't afraid to try new things and make their own unique cuisine.
Let your taste buds be your guide as you venture forth into the world of new ingredients and cuisines. Creating delicious meals is about more

than just following a recipe; it's also about connecting with others over a shared passion and learning new techniques.

The Epicurean Adventure Is Not Over

Learning the basics of cooking is not the end goal, but rather the means to an end. Your development as a cook is an endless voyage of discovery and growth. No matter how much experience you have in the kitchen, there is always more to learn, new skills to acquire, and new flavors to try.

We hope you'll join us on "The Culinary Chronicles: A Journey Through Food and Cooking," where each meal is an opportunity to hone your cooking abilities, explore your culinary imagination, and appreciate the pleasure of preparing delicious food. The options in the kitchen are merely limited by one's knife abilities, fundamental procedures, and the art of seasoning. Happy cooking!

Chapter 4.
A Palate for the Arts:

Explore the intricate world of flavor, focusing on the science, pairing, and creative use of ingredients to elevate your culinary creations.

"Introduction: A Flavor Symphony"

Flavor is the lifeblood of each successful meal when it comes to the culinary arts. It's not simply the taste; rather, it's the intricate interplay of multiple experiences that both fascinate and move us. As we set out on our culinary adventure, we delve deeply into the complex world of flavor, learning its secrets, delving into its scientific underpinnings, becoming experts in the art of pairing, and fully embracing the unlimited inventiveness that can turn even the most humble of materials into something truly spectacular.

: Flavor Science

How we experience flavor is a collaboration between our taste buds and our olfactory senses. Understanding the subtleties that give each ingredient its own character and the ways in which our senses work together to create a symphony of flavors is the subject of this chapter's scientific analysis.

This course delves at the evolutionary significance of the five basic tastes (sweet, sour, salty, bitter, and umami) and how they shape our preferences across a variety of cuisines.

Explore the fascinating world of fragrances and learn how the olfactory system affects our ability to appreciate food's flavor. The aromatic chemicals in herbs, spices, and other ingredients can transform a dish from mediocre to extraordinary, so it's important to learn more about them.

The importance of texture in flavor is often undervalued. We investigate the relationship between texture and flavor by analyzing the effects of a crunchy crust, a smooth sauce, and a well cooked protein.

The Brain's Perception of Flavor: Understand the role of the brain in flavor perception, including the phenomenon of flavor adaptation and how our perceptions can be altered by external stimuli, such as color and plating.

The Science and Practice of Pairing Flavors

The skillful matching of flavors is what separates a good dish from a truly memorable one. In this chapter, we'll learn the fundamentals of taste pairing by delving into the history of food pairings, the science underlying traditional flavor combinations, and the art of creating novel flavor combinations.

Complementary Pairing: Learn how to create balanced and well-rounded flavors by combining foods that have opposite traits. Consider the combination of honey and blue cheese, where the sweetness of the honey balances the sharpness of the cheese.

Enjoy the exciting interaction of flavors by utilizing the contrast technique. Try out new flavor combinations like salty and sweet, like salted caramel or prosciutto-wrapped melon, and see how you like it.

Learn the fine art of flavor balancing by studying the dynamic between sweet, sour, salty, and bitter components. Master the art of balancing flavors by adjusting spice and other ingredients to perfection.

Travel the world through your taste buds as you sample classic combinations from across the world and around the stove. From the classic Italian marriage of tomatoes and basil to the powerful and nuanced flavors of Indian curries, explore the cultural backgrounds that produce distinct flavor combinations.

Ingenious Ingredient Combinations

There is no limit to what may be accomplished with a little ingenuity in the kitchen; both professional and amateur cooks regularly try new approaches, ingredients, and preparations. From fusion cookery to molecular gastronomy, this chapter delves into the innovative ways in which foodstuffs are put to use.

Fusion Cuisine Reimagined: Savor the inventive, fascinating dishes that result when skilled chefs borrow techniques and ingredients from throughout the world. Check out sushi burritos, which fuse Japanese sushi with Mexican flavors, and Korean tacos, which combine Korean BBQ and Mexican street cuisine.

Substituting one ingredient for another is a great way to exercise your ingenuity while cooking. Learn about plant-based substitutes, rediscovered grains, and other cutting-edge culinary goods that can be used to replace conventional ingredients in ways that are both healthy and environmentally responsible.

The importance of texture in the kitchen cannot be overstated. Master the technique of making foods with contrasting textures by combining, for example, crispy, crunchy, smooth, and creamy components. Learn the principles behind making everything from perfectly crisp tempura to silky smooth custard.

Explore the exciting world of molecular gastronomy, where scientific research and culinary artistry meet. Learn how to spherify, gelify, and foam liquids to create interesting new textures and flavors for your dishes and drinks.
In this chapter, we set out on a global culinary journey because culinary exploration has no borders. We explore the diverse flavors,

ingredients, and preparation methods that define different cuisines from the crowded stalls of Southeast Asian street markets to the intimate cafes of Paris.

Immerse yourself in the exotic flavors of Asia with Asian Culinary Wonders. Learn about the wok-tossed creations of the Chinese and the wok-rich flavors of the Japanese. Savour the aromatic spices of the Indian curries. Explore the methods that have made Asian food so influential in the world of cooking.

The sun-kissed coasts of the Mediterranean are the inspiration for the dishes in Mediterranean Marvels, a cookbook that transports readers to a region where olive oil, fresh herbs, and seasonal food are essential ingredients. Taste the robust flavors of Spanish paella, the tangy freshness of Greek salads, the exotic aromas of Moroccan tagines, and the savory pleasures of Italian pasta. Learn the precise balance between simplicity and complexity that characterizes Mediterranean food.

The flavors of Latin America are alive and full of passion, and you may taste them at the Latin American Fiesta. Treat yourself to the savory depth of Mexican mole, the zing of Peruvian ceviche, the heartiness of Argentine stew, and the tropical delights of Caribbean fare. Get a taste of the vibrant and varied cuisines that honor the meeting of indigenous, European, and African cultures.

Discover the history and regional diversity of European food as you delve into the European Elegance section. Explore the world of French pastries, Italian risotto, Spanish tapas, and Eastern European hearty comfort meals. Learn about the traditions, history, and skills that make European cuisine so special.

"The Ingredients' Long Trip from Farm to Table"
To truly appreciate the flavors of food, one must be familiar with its ingredients and their journey from their origins to the kitchen. In this

chapter, we discuss the farm-to-fork philosophy, environmentally friendly methods, and how where food comes from can affect its flavor and freshness.

Embrace the farm-to-table philosophy, which places a premium on using ingredients that are in peak condition when they are consumed. Find out how you can help your community's farmers, cut down on your carbon footprint, and bring together local food producers and buyers.

In this section, we'll delve into the significance of sustainable sourcing and ethical standards in the food industry. Explore the influence of responsible fishing, fair trade methods, and organic farming on the environment and the quality of food. Learn how making ethical decisions can improve the quality and longevity of your meals.

Seasonality and Flavor: Recognize the subtleties and changing flavors of seasonal ingredients.

year. Learn about the advantages of using seasonal vegetables in the kitchen and the room for innovation it provides in the development of tasty and interesting new recipes.

Learn about the notion of terroir, in which the soil, climate, and geography of a particular place affect the taste of a product like wine, cheese, or coffee. Investigate the concept that the flavor of a place is intrinsic to the flavor and quality of its ingredients.

The Science of Seasoning

The art of seasoning extends well beyond just seasoning with salt and pepper. In this chapter, we explore the science behind seasoning by learning about the flavor triangle, achieving a good balance of flavors, and the use of aromatics.

The Flavor Triangle: Learn more about this framework that shows how sweet, sour, salty, and bitter flavors are interconnected. Learn how the right combination of flavors can take a dish to the next level, and how umami may improve the flavor of any dish.

Learn how aromatics like garlic, onions, and fresh herbs add nuanced flavor to your cooking in this in-depth look at the world of seasonings. Learn the tricks of the trade for using aromatics to create depth of flavor in your cooking.

Seasoning can be done with more than just salt and pepper. Learn how different types of seasonings, such as spices, herbs, condiments, and sauces, may completely alter the flavor of a dish. Learn about the impact spices have had on cuisines all throughout the world.

Marination is a scientific process that infuses proteins and other components with flavor; in The Art of Marination, you'll learn all about it. Learn how acids, lipids, and spices play a part in marination and how it may take a dish from good to great.

True culinary artistry entails developing signature recipes that showcase your personal style and interests, but it is also important to have a firm grasp on the science, pairing, and creative use of ingredients. In this section, we'll give you permission to branch out from tried-and-true recipes and try something new.

Embracing Culinary Imagination: Release your inner chef and show the world how much you love to cook. Learn about different ingredients, cooking styles, and methods to make your own special recipes.

Your distinctive meals are a reflection of your personal style and approach to cooking. Learn how to make each dish an opportunity to express your unique sense of style and individuality.

The Joy of Sharing: Share your love for cooking and your unique recipes with friends and family. Learn the ins and outs of hosting and discover how much fun it can be to make your loved ones feel special at a meal you prepared.

What's Next for Flavor and the Culinary Arts

Cultural transitions, technical developments, and varying consumer tastes all have an impact on the world of cuisine. In this chapter, we take a look into the future of flavor, discussing the trends and advancements that are likely to affect how we perceive and prepare food in the future.

Sustainability and Ethical Dining: The demand for sustainability and ethical dining practices continues to grow. Learn about the efforts being made by restaurants and individuals to lessen their environmental impact, recycle their food scraps, and promote ethical sourcing practices.

The sharing of recipes and ingredients from other cultures has broadened the range of flavors available to people all across the world. Learn how intriguing new flavor combinations are being created as a result of cultural fusion and diversity.

Technology is playing an increasingly important role in the evolution of our relationship with food. Explore the exciting new world of high-tech cooking gadgets, applications, and techniques that are changing the way we prepare food.

Sustainable and ethical alternatives to conventional animal products are emerging in the form of plant-based and lab-grown proteins. Learn about the recent advances in alternative proteins that can satisfy a wide range of dietary restrictions.

A Path to Continuous Education

The pursuit of culinary knowledge is a never-ending quest for improvement. The value of lifelong education is emphasized in this chapter, as you are urged to broaden your gastronomic horizons by trying new ingredients and honing your skills.

Cooking may be a source of great pleasure and learning in The Joy of Learning. Learn how books, courses, and the internet can be your constant friends on a lifetime of culinary adventure.

Culinary Adaptation: Don't close yourself off to change and innovation in the kitchen. Learn about and experiment with different cooking methods, ingredients, and cuisines so that your cooking can grow and change throughout time.

conserving Culinary Traditions: While innovation is appreciated, conserving culinary traditions is also vital. Explore your creativity while learning the cultural and historical relevance of the items and methods you use.

The Culinary Chronicles Your Tasty Adventure

Exploring the complex realm of flavor is an introspective adventure that rewards with a more refined palate, a mastery of the science of seasoning, and the assurance to create one's own culinary creations. In this final section, we hope you'll think back on your culinary adventures so far, relish the dishes you've made, and look forward to the exciting new flavors you'll discover in the future.

To put it simply, Your Flavorful Odyssey is a never-ending excursion through a symphony of flavors, scents, and textures. It's a trip that honors originality in the kitchen and the satisfaction of feeding friends and family.

From Kitchen to Table: The kitchen is more than a place to cook; it's also a place to express oneself creatively, to experiment with new recipes, and to find solace in one's favorite foods. Learn the joy of transforming ordinary ingredients into spectacular meals and the delight of sharing them with loved ones over a meal.

The complex realm of flavor offers endless opportunities, and we should embrace them all. As you continue to experiment in the kitchen, keep in mind that each new dish is a chance to hone your techniques, showcase your imagination, and relish the pleasure of cooking.

In "The Culinary Chronicles: A Journey Through Flavor and Creativity," we pay homage to the science of seasoning, the craft of balancing flavors, and the unbounded imagination that turns simple materials into works of culinary art. May your taste buds lead the way, your enthusiasm propel you, and your kitchen serve as the stage for your most delicious adventures.

Chapter 5.
Unleashing Creativity in the Kitchen:

Uncover the secrets of culinary innovation, from fusion cuisine to molecular gastronomy, and learn how to unleash your own creativity in the kitchen.

Introduction: Revealing the Mysteries of Creative Cooking

The best examples of fusion cooking are those that successfully combine elements from several cultures' cooking traditions. In this chapter, we travel the world via food by investigating the origins, guiding principles, and defining features of fusion cooking.

Learn how fusion food evolved from the sharing of ingredients and cooking techniques between nations in The Historical Tapestry of Fusion. Find out how migration, colonization, and trade have contributed to the modern mingling of cuisines.

The Essence of Fusion: Understand the essential concepts of fusion cuisine, where ingredients, techniques, and traditions from different culinary heritages come together to produce unique and fascinating dishes. Find out how some of the most famous fusion recipes are made.

The Art of Balancing: Fusion cooking is a nuanced tango of tastes and aromas. Master the techniques of preparing dishes in a way that pays homage to many cultures while still retaining their own flavors. Learn about the techniques used by chefs to combine ingredients from other cultures to create delicious new recipes.

In the, we'll dive into the science and art of molecular gastronomy.

Molecular gastronomy is an exciting new trend in the culinary world that combines science and art to create extraordinary dishes. In this section, we explore the fascinating realm of molecular gastronomy, exploring its origins, fundamental procedures, and scientific wonders.

Meet Ferran Adrià, Heston Blumenthal, and Grant Achatz, among other "culinary visionaries" who changed the world via their groundbreaking work in molecular gastronomy. Learn about their ground-breaking techniques and ideas in the kitchen.

Learn how molecular gastronomy techniques like spherification, gelification, foaming, and sous-vide cooking work and what makes them so fascinating. Learn how the physical and chemical properties of components can be manipulated with these techniques.

A Scientific Exploration of Flavor and Texture: Investigate the scientific foundations of molecular cooking in great detail. Examine the effects of low temperatures, pressure, and emulsification on the ingredients. Learn how the skill of controlling flavor and texture generates extraordinary culinary experiences.

Nurturing Your Imagination in the Kitchen

Everyone with a love of food and cooking has the potential to be a creative chef. In this chapter, we will discuss how to foster and release your creative potential through openness to exploration, lifelong learning, and individual expression.

Be bold in the kitchen and try new things without worrying about making a mistake. Discover your own unique cooking style by exploring different ingredients, methods, and flavors.

The value of education as a resource for the kitchen cannot be overstated. Learn the value of lifelong education from a variety of sources, including recipes, classes, seminars, and the internet. Discover how expanding your horizons of knowledge can fuel your imagination to new heights.

honor for Tradition: While innovation is welcomed, it's as important to honor culinary customs. Discover how appreciating the cultural context of your components may elevate your imaginative pursuits.

New Trends in Contemporary Food

Changing social mores and scientific breakthroughs have all had an impact on modern cuisine's ongoing development. In this section, we take a look at the ways in which new techniques and ingredients are changing modern cuisine.

Participate in the Farm-to-Table Dining culture, which places a premium on using in-season, locally sourced ingredients procured directly from farmers and producers. Know that this movement encourages newness, sustainability, and a deeper bond between consumers and their food's origins.

Plant-Based Revolution: The emergence of plant-based cuisine is altering the culinary world. Explore the exciting world of plant-based proteins, non-dairy alternatives, and novel vegetable preparations. Investigate the many ways in which plant-based cuisine may accommodate different diets and moral stances.

Molecular Mixology: Much like molecular gastronomy's impact on the culinary world, it has also been felt in the cocktail industry. Explore the frontiers of mixology with molecular cocktails, which feature novel techniques such as burning drinks and making edible garnishes.

Modern restaurants place equal importance on food's aesthetic presentation as it does on its flavor. Examine the aesthetics of contemporary cuisine, which might include the use of bold colors, inventive plating, and the creation of culinary works of art.

Temporary eating establishments known as "pop-up restaurants" allow chefs to test out new ideas in front of a select, adventurous clientele.

Learn about the history of the "pop-up restaurant" and its impact on the modern dining scene.

What's Next in the World of Food

Sustainability, cross-cultural understanding, and technological advancement will shape the menus of the future. Future fascinating trends and developments that will shape the culinary landscape are discussed in this chapter.

The Sustainable Practices movement is having an impact in the food industry as a whole. More and more kitchens are committing to eco-friendly methods like composting leftovers, buying ingredients in season, and sourcing from nearby farms and fisheries.

Fusion cuisine, in which ingredients from multiple cultures are combined, is predicted to continue to flourish as a result of cultural exchange. The sharing of recipes and ingredients across boundaries broadens the range of flavors available to people everywhere.

Technological advances in the kitchen are altering our relationship with food. Professional and amateur cooks alike are rapidly adopting the use of smart kitchen appliances, culinary apps, and precision cooking techniques.

We may anticipate more developments in alternative protein products as the need for plant-based and lab-grown protein sources increases. All people, not only vegetarians and vegans, will benefit from these options because they are more environmentally friendly.

Your Culinary Adventure,
In your pursuit of gastronomic originality, keep in mind that your kitchen is much more than a utilitarian space: it's a place of discovery, inspiration, and possibility. The secrets of culinary innovation, from

fusion cuisine to molecular gastronomy, are yours to explore, adapt, and make your own.

We hope you'll join us on "The Culinary Chronicles: Unveiling Creativity in the Kitchen," an epic cookbook that will take you on a journey across the world of food. This adventure provides the excitement of discovery, the joy of creation, and the independence to make your kitchen a stage for your culinary masterpieces, whether you're a seasoned chef or a passionate home cook. So, let your kitchen become a refuge for culinary inventiveness where your imagination can run wild and flavors can blossom.

Chapter 6.
Culinary Anecdotes:

Hear the personal stories and journeys of renowned chefs, food critics, and culinary entrepreneurs, discovering what drives their passion for food.

The Craft of Cooking

Get to know the chefs, the creative minds behind the dishes. In this chapter, we get to hear their backstories and discover what inspired them to start cooking.

Many chefs get their start in their families' kitchens, where they learn to cook and acquire a passion for the profession. Find out what events inspired them to pursue formal study in the culinary arts.

Every great chef learned their craft from an older cook or was inspired by a famous chef they admired. Examine the enormous influence these teachers have had on their students by learning more about their lives and ideologies.

The Culinary Call: Hear the personal stories of the chefs who made cooking more than a profession. Find out what they went through to achieve their goals.

A Palate for the Past

The way we relate to food is frequently intertwined with significant aspects of our past and present lives. In this section, we delve into the life experiences of those who have made a living doing what they love through the medium of food.

To put it simply, food critics are an essential part of the restaurant industry. Explore how these individuals' tastes developed over time and how they went from being enthusiastic foodies to authoritative critics.

The Pleasure of Exploration: Trying new foods and drinks is a hobby for many people. Find out how these critics and aficionados turned their love of food into rewarding professions that allow them to indulge in their hobby while making a living.

Building Relationships: Sharing a meal is a great way to get to know your neighbors. Hear the experiences of those who have utilized food to bring people together, honor traditions, and forge bonds in their communities.

Culinary Entrepreneurs" Making a Living Doing What They Love

Many people wish they could make a living doing what they love. Successful businesspeople who have turned their passion for food into a profession are profiled in this chapter.

From Home Cook to Restaurateur: Hear the inspiring true tales of home cooks and amateur bakers who turned their passion for food into successful businesses.

Entrepreneurial chefs are frequently the first to introduce novel cooking techniques and ingredients. Find out how these visionaries saw a need in the market and brought forth novel ideas and goods that consumers ate up.

The path of an entrepreneur is fraught with peril and opportunity, and vice versa. Hear how the successes, failures, and lessons learned by these food business owners have shaped their journeys.

Culinary Advocates and Activists: Beyond the Kitchen

Flavor is simply one aspect of food; issues of fairness, sustainability, and morality also play a role. People whose enthusiasm for food has led them to become activists and advocates are profiled in this chapter.

Explore the lives of those who are fighting for a better food system through the stories in Champions of Sustainability. Find out what they're doing to encourage eco-friendly eating, help local farmers, and cut down on food waste.

Food can be used to bring about positive change and to solve societal challenges. Find out more about the people who are working to end food insecurity and provide more chances to underrepresented communities by using food as a tool.

The Moral Search for True Gastronomic Perfection" When it comes to ingredients and methods, some chefs and other food experts have made it their mission to be as conscientious as they are talented. Explore their personal experiences and the impact of their conscientious choices on the culinary world.

"Passing the Flame: Culinary Mentoring and Teaching"

Many successful chefs and restaurateurs feel a strong need to pass on their expertise to the next generation. In this section, we explore the lives of persons who have made a commitment to mentoring and education.

In this episode of The Teacher's Journey, we talk to former chefs who are now educators. Investigate why they feel compelled to share their knowledge with future cooks and foodies.

There are many examples of mentor-apprentice relationships in the realm of food. Find out how influential figures in the lives of famous chefs have influenced their work and outlook. Find out how these connections have impacted the lives of their students.

In many societies, recipes and cooking techniques are passed down from generation to generation. Learn about the lives of those who have made it their mission to ensure that time-tested cooking methods are passed down from generation to generation.

Struggles and Successes - Examples of Fortitude

There are always inspiring tales of grit and determination behind every famous chef. In this section, we hear inspiring accounts of people who have faced adversity and come out on top.

Culinary Dreams and Roadblocks: The route to culinary achievement is seldom free of hurdles. Examine the personal and professional difficulties encountered by chefs, food critics, and business owners in the culinary industry.

Successful people are characterized by their ability to bounce back quickly from setbacks. Listen to the accounts of those who have overcome great odds through sheer willpower, tenacity, and faith.

Any difficulty encountered is a learning experience. Learn how the struggles of successful chefs have influenced their personalities and their jobs.

"Food in the Future: Dreams and Hopes"

Future developments in the food industry will be shaped in large part by the hopes and dreams of those who have devoted their lives to the industry. Here, our protagonists and antagonists take us into the world of tomorrow's food.

Learn about the intriguing sustainability practices, culinary technologies, and new food concepts that our storytellers foresee in "Culinary Innovations on the Horizon."Learn about the hopes and dreams of cooks who want to make a difference in the industry. Find out what they have in mind to make the food sector more environmentally friendly, welcoming, and exciting. Helpful Hints for Future Cooks: Our narrators have invaluable insights to share with aspiring cooks, food critics, restaurant owners, and food activists. Find out what advice they have for people who are interested in exploring the world of food.

Our common love of and appreciation for food transcends language barriers and cultural divides. In this final section, we honor the unifying factor that runs across the experiences of such illustrious cooks, reviewers, businesspeople, and activists as we have thus far.

Food speaks to the human soul regardless of barriers of language and culture. Discover the ways in which our mutual love of food strengthens our bonds with one another and the world. People from many walks of life come together to form the diverse and dynamic community that is the culinary world. Gratitude for a shared experience and

friendship forged by a common interest in dining.

Our Cooking Adventures: The extraordinary adventures and individual experiences we've uncovered here are a tribute to the value of commitment and enthusiasm. In honoring the varied journeys that have brought these people to the culinary arts, we are reminded that the world of food is a rich tapestry of people's tales, tastes, and experiences, bound together by a shared passion for the delectable.

In "The Culinary Chronicles: Where Passions Unfold," we set out on a meaningful journey through the stories of celebrated cooks, food writers, restaurant owners, and food activists. These anecdotes are a gentle reminder that food is much more than a means to an end; it's also a window into other worlds, a platform for expression, and a motor of progress. In honor of these people who have devoted their lives to the culinary arts, let us all take time to savor the tastes of life and the comfort it provides around the table.

Chapter 7.
Celebrations and feasts:

Dive into the world of food celebrations and traditions, from Thanksgiving to Chinese New Year, and learn how to create memorable feasts for special occasions.

A Grateful Thanksgiving Feast

The spirit of thankfulness and community is at the heart of Thanksgiving, a traditional American holiday. In this chapter, we look into the history of Thanksgiving, the classic dishes that grace the table, and the secrets to constructing a flawless Thanksgiving feast.

Examine the origins of Thanksgiving, which may be traced back to the arrival of the Pilgrims in the New World and their first successful harvest. Learn the history of this national holiday that emphasizes thankfulness and camaraderie.

Discover the traditional Thanksgiving dishes that have come to define the holiday, from the roast turkey and mashed potatoes to the savory cranberry sauce and sweet stuffing. Master the methods used to create these delicacies.

Contemporary Spins on Classics: Celebrate the inventive spirit of modern Thanksgiving cuisine with fresh takes on traditional dishes. Learn how modern cooks, both professional and amateur, are reimagining Thanksgiving classics while staying true to the spirit of the event.

Christmas, a Culinary Extravaganza is

Christmas is a magical season, full of bright decorations, heartwarming music, and delicious treats. From Yule logs to gingerbread houses, this chapter delves into the seasonal treats that set the tone for the holiday season.

The Magic of Christmas Feasts: Travel through the Christmas culinary traditions, from the cozy Dickensian English feasts to the lavish multi-course celebrations of Europe. Learn the history and symbolism behind seasonal dishes including Christmas pudding, roasted meats, and fruitcake.

It's no secret that different cultures have different gastronomic customs when it comes to Christmas celebrations. Explore numerous Christmas foods, such as Italian panettone, Spanish turron, and Mexican tamales, that make Christmas a global culinary adventure.

Master the skill of preparing a Christmas feast that reflects the spirit of the season. Find out how to cook a delicious Christmas turkey, make a variety of holiday desserts, and fill your home with the spirit of the season.

Hanukkah, the Festival of Lights and Delights, is discussed in

Celebrating miracles and long-standing customs, Hanukkah is known as the "Festival of Lights." In this section, we explore the traditions and foods that make Hanukkah special, from latkes to sufganiyot.

Learn about the background of Hanukkah, the festival that celebrates the miracle of the menorah that blazed for eight days, in The Miracle of Hanukkah. Find out why the menorah, the game of dreidel, and other customs are so important to the Jewish holiday of Hanukkah.

Learn about the history and significance of Hanukkah's traditional foods, including the crispy potato latke and the jelly-filled sufganiyot. Find out how they're made and learn some interesting new takes on the classic Hanukkah cuisine.

Celebrating with Family dishes: Family dishes are the core of Hanukkah celebrations. Learn the value of passing on tried and true recipes from generation to generation and the joy of experimenting with new flavors.

Diwali, the Festival of Lights and Sweets

Diwali, often known as the "Festival of Lights," is a Hindu festival honoring the triumph of good over evil. The bright and colorful world of Diwali sweets, from jalebi to barfi, is the subject of this chapter.

The Sweetest Festival of the Year: Learn about the history and significance of the Diwali celebration, which includes the giving and receiving of gifts, the lighting of oil lamps, and the use of fireworks. Learn the meaning behind rangoli patterns, puja rites, and the pleasure of giving gifts.

Mithai, or Diwali sweets, are an essential part of the festival. Explore the many varieties of Indian desserts, from the sticky-sweet jalebi to the light and airy rose-flavored gulab jamun. Discover the rich regional variation of Indian mithai as you master the skill of making these delicious delicacies.

Sharing sweets and cooking traditional dishes from one's family is at the center of the Diwali celebration. Hear how food has played a significant role in bringing families together around Diwali and how grandmothers have passed on their recipes.

Traditional Chinese Food for the New Year

The Chinese New Year, or Spring Festival, is a time to honor the coming of a new year along with one's family and one's cultural heritage. From dumplings to longevity noodles, we explore the whole spectrum of Chinese New Year fare in this chapter.

Learn about the significance of certain dishes during the Chinese New Year and how they relate to other customs by reading "The Essence of Chinese New Year." Learn the significance of the dragon and lion dances and the ancestor worship at the Lantern Festival.

The foods eaten during Chinese New Year are full with meaning, especially Dumplings and Other Symbolic Foods. Learn the symbolism behind dishes like whole fish and dumplings, which have meanings related to prosperity and fortune. Find out what they mean and how to make these foods.

Generational Wisdom and Culinary Legacy: Chinese New Year is a time when generations get together to celebrate and pass on culinary wisdom. Listen to accounts about the lasting value of family recipes and the satisfaction of serving them to loved ones.

Easter, the "Feast of Renewal and Rebirth," is discussed in

Easter, a Christian celebration commemorating Jesus' resurrection, is characterized by customs associated with fresh starts and new beginnings. The delicious foods associated with Easter are discussed in this chapter, from lamb to hot cross buns.

The lamb of God and the Easter bunny are just two of the many religious and cultural symbols associated with Easter that you should learn about. Learn about the significance of Easter eggs, the ritual of egg rolling, and the symbolism of hot cross buns.

Many Easter dinners feature lamb as the main course. Learn how to roast luscious lamb with all the sauces and seasonings that make it a symbol of rebirth and refreshment.

Baking sweets such as hot cross buns, simnel cake, and chocolate eggs take center stage during the Easter holiday. Dig into the secrets of making these delicious Easter treats and hear about the customs that have been passed down through the generations.

connected to them.

Day of the Dead: A Celebration of Life and Death,

The Day of the Dead is a Mexican holiday commemorating and paying tribute to ancestors and other departed loved ones. From sugar skulls to pan de muerto, this chapter delves into the delicious Da de los Muertos food customs.

Da de los Muertos, often known as "The Day of the Dead," is a Mexican holiday celebrated on November 2nd that combines indigenous and Catholic rituals to remember and honor the dead. Learn about the significance of marigolds, ofrendas (altars), and offering food and drink to the dead.

Learn more about the significance of sugar skulls and calacas to the celebration of Dia de los Muertos in Sugar Skulls and Calacas. Find out what these calacas (skeleton figures) mean in terms of the celebration's history and culture.

Pan de Muerto and Family Recipes: Pan de muerto, a sweet, anise-flavored bread covered with bone-shaped decorations, is a major component of Día de los Muertos. Learn the ins and outs of making pan de muerto and why it's so important to pass along family recipes for this holiday.

Planning Extraordinary Celebration Meals

Making a festive meal that everyone will remember is a skill that blends experience and innovation. Herein, we provide instruction on how to cook memorable feasts appropriate for every occasion worthy of commemoration, whether it is a special event, a family reunion, or a personal achievement.

"Setting the Table for Celebration" delves into the finer points of creating an elegant atmosphere for a meal. Discover what it takes to set the mood for a joyous celebration that everyone can enjoy.

Learn the tricks of the trade that will take your holiday cooking to the next level. We offer advice to help you cook delicious meals, from roasting a perfect turkey to making beautiful desserts.

Celebrations provide an excellent setting for Innovative Twists on Tradition. Find out how to give your food a creative twist without ignoring the traditions and tastes that make the event special.

Preserving Culinary customs: Cherish family recipes and cultural customs by handing them on to future generations. The significance of passing along recipes and the memories that accompany them is discussed.

The Happiness of Gathering Together to Celebrate

The fabric of celebrations is woven from more than just the food they provide. In this section, we consider how much pleasure people of many backgrounds can derive from being together to celebrate and partake in common culinary practices.

Celebrations are a manifestation of our fundamental yearnings for social interaction and emotional fulfillment. Explore the emotional and cultural value of gathering together on significant occasions.

Food is the common language of celebration, so sharing a meal together is a great way to bring people together. Learn how sharing a meal, a tradition, or a story can bring people closer together and leave them with fond memories for years to come.

The celebration of life's major moments is a time-honored tradition. Examining the foods associated with significant life events and the memories they evoke, such as birthdays, weddings, and graduations.

Making Delicious Memories

As our exploration of the world's culinary holidays and customs comes to a close, we take stock of the many ways in which food and family have shaped our most cherished memories. In this final section, we toast the skill of creating delectable recollections.

Culinary Traditions as Time Capsules: Culinary traditions have the capacity to take us back in time, evoking cherished memories and conserving the essence of our culture and heritage. Learn more about the way our food habits can tell the story of our past.

To paraphrase the subtitle, "The Art of Storytelling Through Food," every dish has a backstory, and every meal is a tale just waiting to be told. Learn how our dishes take on new meaning thanks to the stories we tell about them.

The Legacy of Celebratory Feasts: The food customs we adopt now will be the ones we leave behind for the future. Examine the value of both continuing and establishing new customs.

Throughout "Celebrating with Food: Crafting Memorable Feasts for Special Occasions," we've sampled the culinary delights that are a hallmark of festivities in many different cultures. Every celebration is a celebration of the strength of history, imagination, and community. May the meals you prepare and the traditions you start be a reflection of how much you value family, friends, and the delicious foods that bring us all together.

Chapter 8.
Eating in a Sustainable Way:

Discuss the importance of sustainability in the culinary world, exploring eco-friendly practices, ethical sourcing, and reducing food waste.

The Immediate Need for Sustainability

The globe is at a juncture where unprecedented environmental challenges must be met. Understanding the far-reaching effects of our decisions as consumers and producers, this chapter delves into the urgent need for sustainability in the culinary world.

Examine the environmental effects of food production, including carbon emissions, deforestation, and habitat loss, in The Culinary Ecological Footprint. Realize how critical it is to lessen our negative impact on the environment while cooking.

Food insecurity, hunger, and unequal access to resources are just few of the hallmarks of the worldwide food crisis, which you must grasp in order to understand the full extent of the situation. Find out why sustainability is a crucial element of the answer.

It's not a fad to care about the environment; it's the right thing to do. Fair work standards, animal welfare, and social responsibility are just a few of the ethical concerns that motivate sustainable decisions.

Sustainable Sourcing: Putting Moral Options on the Menu is of this book. Sustainable sourcing is the foundation of a responsible culinary sector. From the farm to the table, we investigate the methods that support ethical decisions in this chapter.

Learn how ethical decisions made at any point in the process may have a dramatic effect on the final product, from the farm to your plate.

Local sourcing is essential to environmental responsibility. Find out how helping out your neighborhood's farmers and craftsmen can help cut down on your carbon footprint and boost your community's economy.

Responsible fishing and aquaculture are just two examples of how the seafood industry may be more sustainable under the Sustainable Seafood section. Realize the significance of maintaining healthy marine ecosystems and protecting our oceans.

A increasing world population can be fed without depleting the planet's resources if sustainable agriculture is practiced. This chapter delves into the ideas and technologies behind environmentally friendly farming methods.

Soil health, biodiversity, and carbon sequestration are the three main tenets of regenerative agriculture, which you'll learn about in this article. Find out how this method can help the environment and slow global warming.

Organic farming is a sustainable method because it does not use any artificial inputs like pesticides or fertilizers. Investigate the positive effects that organic farming has on both ecosystems and human health.

Urban Farming and Vertical Agriculture: Urban farming and vertical agriculture offer creative solutions to food production, especially in urban settings. Get educated on how adopting these procedures can lessen the distance food travels and increase food safety.

The battle against food waste is discussed in

One of the most important aspects of sustainability is lowering food waste rates. In this chapter, we look at the shocking scale of food waste, the factors that contribute to it, and the innovative approaches taken to address this worldwide issue.

An Alarmed Look at Food Waste: Learn the scope of the problem of wasted food around the world, from production to consumption. Learn about the effects that this widespread problem has on people's lives and the world around them.

Food waste has many reasons, including overproduction, consumer behavior, and false beliefs about food safety, all of which must be investigated. Discover the role that each player in the food supply chain plays in wasting food.

Explore novel approaches and projects to the problem of food waste, from the recycling of leftovers to the development of delicious new dishes from scraps of edible material.

The Green Kitchen: Sustainable Practices for the Food Service Industry is discussed in When it comes to advocating for environmentally responsible practices in the food industry, restaurants are invaluable. This chapter delves into the ways in which the culinary industry is becoming more environmentally conscious.

Learn about the growing trend of "green" eateries that make an effort to use environmentally responsible practices. Find out more about methods like using seasonal and locally sourced ingredients, recycling, and using appliances that use less energy.

To that end, one pressing issue for the restaurant industry is how to Reduce Food Waste in the Kitchen. Explore the methods used by chefs to reduce food waste, such as strategic menu planning, careful stocking, and measured servings.

Realize why it's crucial for eateries to practice sustainable sourcing (Sustainable Sourcing on the Menu). Learn how chefs are engaging with local farmers, fishers, and producers to create seasonal and sustainable dishes.

The Conscientious Shopper: Choosing Healthful, Long-Lasting Foods

The first step toward a more sustainable culinary future is making well-informed decisions as a customer. In this section, we equip readers with the knowledge and skills they need to make environmentally responsible food choices in the grocery store, in the kitchen, and at the table.

You can be a more conscientious consumer by learning to purchase sustainably by paying attention to things like product packaging, country of origin, and environmental labeling.

Sustainable Cooking strategies: Discover sustainable cooking strategies that decrease waste, conserve energy, and make the most of ingredients. Learn new skills in the kitchen, such canning and "nose-to-tail" cuisine.

Learn how to eat out responsibly by frequenting establishments that place a premium on environmental responsibility and choosing sustainable food selections.

Sustainability through Culinary Education

Education in the culinary arts is crucial to the development of the sector as a whole. In this chapter, we discuss the significance of sustainability in culinary education and the power of the next generation of chefs to effect positive change.

Sustainable Culinary Curricula: Research how sustainability is being taught in culinary programs, including topics like ethical sourcing, waste minimization, and more.

The Duty of Tomorrow's Cooks: Learn the role that aspiring chefs and cooks may play in promoting environmental stewardship. Find out how they may be agents of change in their field, shape consumer preferences, and pioneer environmentally responsible dining options.

Technology and sustainability make a formidable team, as discussed in.

When it comes to achieving sustainability, technology is a game-changer. In this chapter, we delve into the technical breakthroughs that are fostering a more sustainable culinary industry.

Learn how precision agriculture, data analytics, and automation are revolutionizing sustainable farming by improving crop yields, decreasing input costs, and streamlining operations.

The significance of digital platforms and apps in minimizing food waste is investigated, including the redistribution of surplus food and the use of smart inventory management systems.

Sustainable Kitchen Appliances and Gadgets: Discover how to cut down on your water and power usage in the kitchen by using eco-friendly appliances and gadgets.

The Future of Food on a Sustainable Planet,

Looking ahead, there is a lot of hope and opportunity in the future of sustainable cooking. In this chapter, we discuss our hopes for the future of sustainable cuisine and the part that each of us can play in making that future a reality.

The Future We Want to See: Imagine a day in the future when all areas of the food industry, from sourcing to waste management, are committed to sustainability. Investigate the positive effects on ecosystems, societies, and human health that may result.

Recognize that achieving sustainability is a shared responsibility that must include organizations of all sizes and levels of government. Learn how progress may be made toward sustainability through policy shifts and international collaboration.

Recognize the significance of individual actions in fostering sustainability. It's important to make decisions that have an impact, whether it's choosing to buy from local farms, cutting down on food waste at home, or lobbying for sustainable practices.

Sustainability's Gastronomic Heirlooms"

This final section offers some thoughts on the sustainable cuisine legacy. We honor the chefs, farmers, activists, and others who have promoted environmentally responsible methods and made significant contributions to the world of food.

The Lasting Impact of Sustainability Leaders: Honor the eco-heroes who have spent their lives spreading the word about healthy eating and cooking. Discover the enduring impact they have made on the industry and the contributions they made.

Learn how sustainable practices can be used to create new interpretations of old culinary traditions. Investigate how traditions and new ideas can coexist for the betterment of food in the long run.

As we wrap off our investigation into eco-friendly cooking practices, we are aware that we have only just begun our trip. Accept the duty of carrying on the legacy of sustainability and creating a better, more sustainable future for everyone.

For the purpose of "The Sustainable Plate: Nourishing the Future," we have set out on a serious expedition into the realm of sustainable cuisine. The importance of sustainability in determining the future of food has been highlighted by this voyage. Every action we take as people, customers, and professionals may contribute to a more sustainable and resilient food system, as we are reminded when we recognize the significance of eco-friendly practices, ethical sourcing, and decreasing food waste. We hope that this voyage will encourage us to take better care of our planet and to relish the tastes of a more sustainable future.

Chapter 9.
Cooking Diaries:

Document your own culinary journey and experiences, with space for personal recipes, tasting notes, and reflections on your growth as a cook.

The A Taste-Testing Adventure

The first step on any culinary adventure is always a new taste. In this section, I'll share some of the earliest memories I have with the foods and flavors that sparked my interest in cooking.

Early Food Memories delves into the formative experiences with food that have stayed with you throughout your life. Learn about the meetings and meals that inspired my love of cooking and eating.

Explore the flavors that have had the most impact on my tastebuds by reading Influential Flavors. Learn about the wide range of flavors that have inspired my culinary adventures, from the familiarity of classic recipes to the intrigue of exotic spices.

In First Kitchen Adventures, I'll take you along on my culinary journey back to my earliest days of experimentation. Here you can read about my earliest culinary experiments and the lessons I learned from them.

Culinary Training and Apprenticeship

Getting trained to cook is a major step along the way. In this section, I discuss the mentors and resources that have helped me along the way in my journey of academic and informal culinary education.

Take a look at my Formal Culinary Training to learn more about the time I spent in restaurants, workshops, and apprenticeships. Find out how I've improved my abilities and knowledge of cooking through formal study.

Mentors and Influences: Discover the chefs and culinary personalities who have influenced and inspired me along the way. Explore the advice and counsel I've received from my various chefs of experience, both famous and otherwise, both in and out of the kitchen.

Cookbooks, Weblogs, and Other Virtual Materials: Culinary education happens everywhere, not just in a classroom. In this post, I'll go over the books, websites, and blogs that have helped me become a better cook and given me numerous ideas.

A Gastronomic Exploration of the World

Experiencing new flavors is an adventure in and of itself. In this section, I discuss how my exposure to many cuisines and civilizations has broadened my culinary horizons.

Culinary Travels: Embark on a tour to numerous destinations throughout the globe. I discuss my adventures in discovering new and exciting foods from around the world at venues ranging from crowded food markets to modest street stalls.

Experience the rich variety of flavors found in cuisines from around the world with Flavors of the World. I'll take you on a journey around the world's cuisines, from the Moroccan spice souks to the sushi restaurants of Japan, explaining the regional specialties and regional cooking methods I've discovered along the way.

The cultural lessons I've received from my culinary travels go beyond the dishes themselves. Insight into the culture, history, and customs of a place can be gained through its cuisine.

My Kitchen Chronicles, Rookie Cook to Natural Born Chef

My home kitchen is where my exploration of food and cooking really begins. Here I detail how my cooking has progressed from its rudimentary origins to its present state of sophistication.

Every chef has made a few rookie mistakes in the kitchen. Some of my kitchen blunders have been both funny and humbling, and I'll explain how I learnt from them.

Check out the recipes I've perfected and give some thought to the dishes I've come to call "signature." I'll share the dishes that best represent my cooking philosophy, from tried-and-true standards to daring new creations.

Memorable dinner parties, family get-togethers, and the pride I had after learning new skills are just a few of the highlights of my career in the kitchen that I'd like to look back on as I write this.

Seasonal Delights: A Year of Food for Thought is the and final .

The gastronomic journey is intimately related to the seasons. In this reflect on a year's worth of food, from the first tastes of spring to the cozy meals of winter.

Spring Awakening: I rejoice in the fresh tastes of spring when the earth awakens from its winter slumber. Find out what foods and ingredients are typical at this time of year.

Summer Bounty: Summer is a season of plenty. Taste the summer with me as we feast on fresh produce, vibrant vegetables, and mouthwatering grilled treats.

As the weather cools and the leaves turn, I indulge in some of autumn's most comforting foods in Autumn Harvest. I'll explain why I adore autumnal dishes, from pumpkin-spiced sweets to warming stews.

Winter Comfort: The colder months demand for warm and comforting foods. Taste your way through the winter season with hearty stews, tender roasts, and sweet desserts.

Sharing culinary moments is the focus of"The Art of Entertaining."

Sharing a meal is one of life's greatest pleasures. In this I share stories about my experiences as an entertainer, host, and chef for friends and family.

Feel the satisfaction of hosting a dinner party or other social gathering. Find out how the people in my life and the experiences we shared together have shaped my approach to cooking.

Special Occasions: Savor the holidays and special days I've commemorated with delicious creations and cherished customs. Learn the traditions and practices surrounding these meals.

"Food as Connection" delves on the role that eating together has played in bringing people closer together and making memories that will last a lifetime. I'll tell tales of happy times spent with friends and family over a delicious supper.

Cooking Thoughts: Savoring the Flavors of Life is discussed in

Savoring a meal is a form of culinary art. In this section, I discuss the sensory experiences that have shaped my approach to food and dining.

Read my sensory notes and learn about the fine art of taste. I'll spill the beans on how dishes really smell, what they taste like, and how they feel in your mouth.

Wine, cheese, and food pairings have been the subject of countless "Pairing Adventures." Discover the delicious combos I've discovered and the ideas underlying harmonizing flavors.

Beyond the realm of taste, I investigate other sensory experiences that elevate dining occasions. I am happy to discuss the finer points of dining with you, from the aesthetic appeal of a beautifully presented meal to the pleasure of a wonderfully textured bite.

A Cooking Space in Transition - Environmental Impact

and the Art of Mindful Cooking

Embracing sustainability and mindful cooking are integral parts of the culinary journey. In this section, I discuss my dedication to sustainability, fair trade, and waste-free eating. Sustainable Cooking methods: Dive into the sustainable cooking methods that have been important to my culinary path. Learn about the eco-friendly practices that define my kitchen, from my commitment to zero food waste to my advocacy for local farmers.

The use of organic foods, promotion of fair trade, and concern for the well-being of animals are only a few examples of my commitment to ethical sourcing.

A major issue in the culinary industry is the excessive amount of food that is thrown out every year. Find out how I've been trying to cut down on food waste through careful portioning, inventive cooking, and careful storing.

Next up on our culinary adventure: our hopes and dreams for the future. As I wrap out this record, I can't help but think about the delicious adventures that lie ahead. In this section, I discuss the hopes, dreams, and future developments that will guide me along my chosen culinary route.

I discuss the uncharted regions of the culinary world that I can't wait to explore in the future in Uncharted Culinary Territories. My ultimate foodie goals, from trying out exotic cuisines to mastering cutting-edge techniques, are all laid out here.

Recognize the cooks, writers, and media figures who have influenced me throughout the years. Find out what motivates my never-ending quest for new gastronomic experiences. Discover my plans for documenting, instructing, and inspiring people with my culinary adventures in Sharing the Culinary Journey. Learn about my plans to give back to the food industry.

A Culinary Legacy - Recording the Trip

In this final chapter, I underline the value of chronicling one's culinary experience. Think about why it's important to record your thoughts, memories, and favorite recipes for posterity.

Respect the fact that every cook leaves behind something delicious, be it a recipe, a story, or a tradition. Learn the value of recording this history for future generations. Even though I've reached this point in writing about my gastronomic adventures, I'm not stopping here. Each step brings the promise of new experiences, flavors, and opportunities for development, and I eagerly anticipate them.

We've set out on a very introspective journey in "My Culinary Journey: A Documentation of Tastes and Tales," exploring the tastes, customs, and experiences that have influenced my culinary development. This adventure is a celebration of the ability of food to bind us to our pasts, our communities, and the sheer delight of making something new. I record my culinary exploits in the hopes that they would encourage others to try new things and learn from their mistakes, just as I have done throughout my life.

Chapter 10.
Food in the Future:

Examine emerging trends and technologies shaping the future of food and cooking, including food tech, farm-to-table movements, and innovative dining experiences.

Introduction: A Taste of Tomorrow - New Developments in the Food Industry and Cooking Technology

The Culinary Evolution Driven by the Food Tech Revolution

The cultivation, processing, and consumption of our food are all being revolutionized by technological advances. The technologies that are changing the food industry are the focus of this chapter as we investigate the food tech revolution.

Learn about the innovative gadgets, applications, and linked devices that are changing the way we cook and eat in "The Digital Kitchen." Learn more about the smart kitchen of the future, from precise cooking gear to recipe management apps.

The Power of AI: AI is revolutionizing the culinary arts by facilitating the development of new dishes and recipes. Find out how things like AI-powered recipe generators, customized meal planning, and food-focused chatbots are changing the way we eat.

3D Food Printing: Step into the realm of layered delicious delights made possible by 3D printing. Find out how this tech can be used to make one-of-a-kind meals, solve the problem of food scarcity, and help the environment.

The Farm-to-Table Movement: Reclaiming Our Roots

The farm-to-table movement is a reflection of the increasing demand for food that is produced sustainably and ethically. In this chapter, we look at how this trend will affect the food industry in the future.

The Farm-to-Table Philosophy: Learn about the ideas behind this movement that promotes openness, ecological responsibility, and a personal relationship between food producers and their customers.

Local Food Hubs and Farmers' Markets: Discover the relevance of local food hubs and farmers' markets in the farm-to-table movement. Learn more about the positive effects that helping local farmers can have on your community.

Examine how Urban Farming and Vertical Agriculture are allowing for the cultivation of fresh produce in urban cores. Find out how these technological advancements are facilitating food security and decreasing food miles.

Creative Meals That Go Beyond the Traditional

Dining is no longer just about the food; it's about the full experience. In this section, we explore the exciting world of multisensory restaurants.

Gastronomic tourism, in which visitors seek out local culinary traditions, is on the rise. Investigate the influence that eating one's way throughout the world has on both economics and cultures.

All the senses are used in multi-sensory dining, which results in delicious and memorable meals. Explore the realm of sensory-rich dining, which includes everything from pop-up meals with a twist to restaurants that use technology in interesting ways.

The popularity of "experimental culinary concepts" like "dining in the dark" and "food pairing with virtual reality" attests to this trend. Learn how these unique events push the envelope of what diners can expect from their food.

The Rise of the Plant-Based Diet: Rethinking the Dinner Table

The shift toward plant-based diets is altering our cultural understanding of nourishment. In this chapter, we look at how the growing popularity of vegetarian and vegan diets is altering the food industry.

The Increasing Popularity of Plant-Based Diets Learn about the health, environmental, and animal-welfare benefits of switching to a plant-based diet. Learn about the spectrum of vegetarian and vegan diets.

Vegan alternatives to meat and dairy are being developed thanks to technological advances in the plant-based food industry, which you should look into. Discover the game-changing items that are available now, from plant-based cheeses to lab-grown meat.

Investigate how vegetarian and vegan dishes have made their way onto restaurant menus. Learn how some of the world's best chefs are upending the concept of fine dining with their inventive plant-based menus.

The Future of Sustainably Sourced Food

The future of cooking and eating is inherently tied to sustainability. In this chapter, we investigate the numerous ways in which sustainability is becoming important to culinary practices.

Responsible fishing and aquaculture techniques are a big part of the sustainable seafood movement, which aims to preserve marine ecosystems so that future generations can enjoy seafood as much as we do now.

Examine how the idea of a "circular economy" can be applied to the food industry. Find out about programs that aim to make better use of leftovers and dispose of less edible food.

Learn the techniques of Zero-Waste Cooking, which center on making full use of each and every portion of the ingredients used in a dish. Discover innovative zero-waste approaches to cooking and eating.

Fusion Food and Beyond at a Crossroads of Cultures

A new definition of global cuisine is emerging at the intersections of cultures, traditions, and ingredients. Fusion food and cultural culinary exchange are the topics of this chapter.

Explore the exciting world of fusion cuisine, a style of cooking in which food and methods from several cultures are brought together. Taste the diverse and exciting flavors that have emerged from this melting pot of cuisine.

Learn the differences between cultural appropriation and cultural appreciation, especially as they pertain to fusion cooking. Learn how some cooks are balancing

distinction between respecting and stealing from past cultures.

worldwide Culinary Exchange: Celebrate the worldwide culinary exchange, where chefs and food aficionados are sharing flavors and methods across borders. Find out more about the celebrations, events, and partnerships that highlight this gastronomic interchange.

From the Farm to the Table: The Future of Food Education

Education about food and where it comes from is changing to better equip people to make healthy decisions. We look into the future of food education in this chapter.

The importance of food literacy and how it helps create well-informed shoppers is covered. Learn more about the available resources whose goals include informing people about the history and significance of the food they eat.

Examine the development of sustainable cooking workshops that show students how to prepare tasty food while leaving less of an impact on the environment.

Food as a Tool for Change: Learn how food can be used to effect positive social change. Find out how food-related initiatives like these help people gain agency, advance social justice, and combat problems like food deserts and hunger.

New Cooking Methods: Creating a Foodie Revolution

New ideas and methods are always being tested in the kitchen, expanding the boundaries of what is possible in the culinary world. Discover the cutting-edge cooking methods that are changing the culinary landscape in this chapter.

Explore the fascinating fields of molecular gastronomy and sous vide cooking in this in-depth guide. Find out how these methods have altered professional kitchens and the way we cook at home.

Examine the resurgence of time-honored practices like fermentation and food preservation (Fermentation and Preservation). Learn how these techniques improve the flavor of food and help to keep it around for the long haul.

Learn about the potential of indoor vertical farms and lab-grown meat in the Future of Food Production. Learn how these strategies are tackling problems like resource depletion and climate change.

The Mutual Benefits of Food and Technology.

There is a mutually beneficial interaction between the food industry and the technological sector. In this chapter, we look at how new tools are changing the way we eat.

Blockchain's potential in the food supply chain is explored in a new book. Discover how it may improve information sharing, tracking, and the security of food supplies.

Augmented Reality Dining: Step into the realm of augmented reality dining, where technology transforms the dining experience. Examine the ways in which augmented reality (AR) improves food presentation, visual appeal, and narrative.

Recognize the value of online food communities and other social media for exchanging tips and tricks in the kitchen and general foodie lore. Investigate how the Internet has altered the culinary world.

Food for Thought, Action, and the Earth

We conclude our survey of recent developments in the kitchen by considering the value of a heightened awareness of what goes into our food. In this final section, we consider how food sustains not only our physical selves, but also our mental health and the health of the earth.

Mindful Eating and Food Mindfulness: Adopt the practices of mindful eating and food mindfulness, which call on us to pay closer attention to the food we consume, develop a stronger emotional connection to our meals, and learn more about the stories behind the ingredients.

Recognize that we each have a duty in the kitchen to make decisions that support sustainability, ethical sourcing, and less food waste. Find out how small changes can add up to big results.
Think about the legacy you're leaving behind in the kitchen for the next generation. The decisions we make now will have lasting effects on the way future generations eat and cook.

In "A Taste of Tomorrow: Emerging Trends and Technologies in Food and Cooking," we set out on a trip through the culinary breakthroughs and movements that are defining the future of food. This research has opened my eyes to a new world where innovation at the intersection of technology, sustainability, and the arts is reshaping the culinary scene. May we all, as we rejoice in the farm-to-table movement, try new culinary creations, and appreciate the promise of food technology, do so with a feeling of culinary conscience, mindful of the impact our eating habits have on our health and the health of the world we live in.

The Role of Food in Shaping Cultural Identity

Beyond its practical use as fuel, food has a profound impact on our lives, binding us to our heritage and revealing our cultural character. There is a complex, ever-changing, and extremely important link between cuisine and culture. Exploring the profound connections between our food and our identities, this article explores the many ways in which food is essential in creating and maintaining cultural identity.

Flavors from Around the World:

The distinctive smells, tastes, and textures of traditional cuisine are frequently a means of communicating and expressing cultural identity. The unique culinary traditions of every people are a reflection of their rich history, varied landscapes, temperate zones, and the imaginations of their ancestors. Consider the diverse array of Asian cuisines; each one offers a unique sensory experience because to the expert blending of herbs, spices, and cooking methods. Every dish reflects a different culture and time period, from the spicy Indian curries to the delicate Japanese sushi.

Similarly, there is a great deal of variation in the culinary traditions across Europe, from the rustic elegance of French cooking to the robust stews of Eastern Europe. One way that cultures are passed down through the years is through the utilization of traditional recipes and local ingredients. In this sense, the cuisine of a people becomes an enduring story about their identity and history told via its flavors.

Customs for Congregation:

As a unifying and communal symbol, food plays an essential role in many cultural festivities and rituals. From religious ceremonies to family reunions, shared meals are frequently the highlight of the event. In addition to strengthening cultural bonds, these shared experiences allow for the transmission of customs from one age to the next.

Take the American Thanksgiving dinner as an example; it is a time for families to gather around a table that has deep cultural and historical roots. Traditional dishes from the early days of colonization, which combined Native American and European flavors, include turkey, cranberry sauce, and pumpkin pie. A sense of community and shared history is fostered through the ritual of making and sharing these particular meals.

Communicating in the Kitchen:

There are no such things as language or cultural barriers when it comes to food. Making and eating traditional foods is like sending a message about who you are without ever saying a word. For instance, preparing and sharing a dish of Italian pasta or Japanese sushi demonstrates a profound affinity for one's history and a resolve to maintain culinary traditions in a way that words alone cannot express.

One way that people in many cultures stay connected to their heritage is via the culinary traditions that have been passed down through the generations. A sense of community, shared values, and culinary traditions are often passed down through generations in the kitchen.

Cooking and sharing food is a way for people to take part in the story of their culture.

Self-Determination in the Routine:

The everyday decisions we make regarding what to eat also play a part in the continuing building of cultural identity, just as big festivals and rituals do. Cultural traditions and values as well as regional ingredient availability impact the foods we choose to eat on a daily basis. The bread one chooses in France, the rice one eats in Asia, or the tortillas one makes in Mexico all contribute to one's cultural identity.

Another way that cultural attitudes about time, leisure, and social connection are reflected in food is how it is prepared and consumed. Example: Some Western countries are known for their fast-paced, on-the-go lifestyles, in contrast to the Mediterranean tradition of the unhurried, communal lunch. Cultural values and priorities are shown by these different ways of eating.

The Evolution of Culture and Fusion of Cuisine:

As with every aspect of a people's identity, their culinary practices change and develop with time. One way in which cuisine can become a living mirror of cultural change is through the practice of culinary fusion. New and intriguing culinary experiences are born from the creative fusion of culinary traditions when societies interact and cultures intermingle.

Think about fusion cuisine in big places like London or New York, where different types of food come together to make new, exciting meals that don't fit neatly into any one category. Cooking with a variety of products and methods from other cultures not only makes for tasty food, but it also represents how interdependent we all are.

Affirming and Strengthening the Role of Food:

As a sign of strength in the face of adversity, food can withstand cultural integration efforts. When faced with colonization or political turmoil, holding on to traditional eating practices becomes a powerful form of resistance, a way to stand up for cultural identity.

In North America, for example, indigenous communities have maintained their culinary traditions through generations of cultural persecution by consuming traditional cuisine. A strong connection to ancestral ways of life and a declaration of identity are both fostered via the making and eating of traditional cuisine.

In summary:

Food shines as a colorful thread in the vast fabric of human experience, connecting our histories, present lives, and future aspirations. Food has an intricate and multi-faceted role in cultural identity formation, including gathering rituals, non-verbal communication, everyday decisions, culinary fusion, and acts of resistance.

We honor our common heritage and individuality in the tastes, smells, and textures of our traditional foods. Food is more than just fuel; it's a powerful representation of our identity, a communal experience that unites us, and a cultural heritage that has been passed down through the years. Sharing a meal together allows us to taste the full spectrum of our cultural identities while also engaging in a form of communication that goes beyond national boundaries and gets to the heart of what it is to be human.

Impact of geographical and climatic factors on food choices.

Around the globe, you can find cuisines that reflect the wide variety of landscapes and climates. The varied landscapes, ranging from verdant rainforests to frozen tundras, influence not just the local flora and fauna but also the culinary habits and preferences of the indigenous peoples that live there. Agricultural methods, culinary traditions, and nutritional preferences have all been shaped by the intricate dance of climate, geography, and food choices that has unfolded throughout human history.

Ample Farmland and Limited Farming Resources:

What crops do well in one area may not do so in another due to differences in topography and soil composition. One way to measure an area's potential for agriculture is by looking at its amount of arable land, water resources, and sunshine. In areas that receive enough of rain and have good soil, many different crops may be grown, which means that people in those areas eat a lot of different foods.

Consider the Nile River's alluvial plains in Egypt. Many different crops, such as cereals, fruits, and vegetables, have been cultivated on the nutrient-rich soil that the river's yearly floods deposits. Wheat, barley, dates, and a variety of vegetables are staples in the traditional Egyptian cuisine, which has been formed by the richness of these agricultural resources.

Conversely, fewer agricultural possibilities may be present in places that experience dry or semi-dry conditions. One of the biggest problems in growing crops is the lack of water. People in these regions have their own distinct culinary traditions since they have always grown crops that can withstand drought and have altered their farming methods accordingly.

Different Climate Zones and Their Impact on Cuisine:

Climate, particularly patterns of precipitation and temperature, is a major factor in dictating which plant and animal species can survive in a given area. Because of this, the locals' food preferences are affected by the weather. Climate zones, which can be classified as tropical, subtropical, temperate, or arctic, have a significant effect on the ingredients that are available and the main dishes that make up a cuisine.

Fruits, vegetables, and spices thrive in tropical climates due to the regularly high temperatures. Tropical fruits like pineapples, mangoes, and bananas, along with a variety of fragrant herbs and spices like ginger, chili peppers, and lemongrass, give Southeast Asian dishes their distinctive flavors. Spicy foods are the main attraction, reflecting the hot weather in the food.

A wider range of temperature changes is observed in temperate locations with different seasons. Seasonal availability of fresh produce and the kinds of crops that can be cultivated are both affected by this variability. The use of seasonal ingredients in European cuisines is a reflection of the influence of temperate climates on culinary preferences. The gastronomic calendar follows the seasons, from winter's substantial soups to summer's crisp salads.

The Sea's Impact on Seafood:

Seafood availability in coastal areas is also influenced by geography, which limits the kinds of crops that can be produced on land. Seas, lakes, and oceans bring a special mix of ingredients to the dishes prepared there. The abundance of marine life provides coastal communities with a foundation upon which to build unique culinary traditions.

The coastal regions of Japan are home to a wide variety of seafood since they are situated where the warm and cold currents of the Pacific Ocean meet. The cultural importance of the ocean and its offerings are reflected in the seafood-based dishes that are important to Japanese cuisine, such as sushi and sashimi. The foundation of a diet that is praised for its health benefits and culinary richness in

Mediterranean coastal locations is the quantity of seafood, together with olive oil, fresh vegetables, and aromatic herbs.

Adaptation in Extreme Conditions:

People living in extreme conditions, such as deserts, high-altitude plateaus, or icy tundras, have been creative when it comes to finding and keeping food. In times of resource shortage, people typically turn to long-standing cultural traditions for inspiration in the kitchen.

For example, in order to survive in the Arctic's cold, herbless climate, the Inuit have long depended on fishing and hunting marine creatures. They survive the long, cold winters by eating mostly seal, whale, and fish, and they preserve their food using ancient ways like fermenting and freezing.

Culinary practices have developed to maximize the use of scarce water in dry places, such as the Middle East. North African couscous and Levantine falafel are examples of dishes that highlight the inventive use of drought-resistant crops and preservation of components that require a lot of water.

Fusion of Cuisines and Globalization:

In today's age of globalization, the influence of climate and geography on dietary preferences is complex and multi-faceted. Modern innovations in transportation and communication have made it easier for ingredients to go across international borders, resulting in the blending of different culinary traditions and the emergence of culinary fusion.

People in urban areas all around the world can now shop at a global pantry, which opens up a whole new world of ingredients to home cooks and chefs. New and exciting meals with ingredients and techniques borrowed from all around the world have emerged as a result of fusion cuisine, a merging of different culinary traditions. Restaurants in vibrant, multicultural cities like New York and Tokyo provide a global tapestry of flavors, reflecting the ethnic and cultural diversity of their customers and chefs.

Nutrition and Health Habits:

The influence of climate and geography on dietary choices is highly related to health and wellbeing, going beyond mere tradition and flavor. There is a strong correlation between the nutritional demands of a certain area and the traditional diets that have developed there. For instance, cardiovascular health is just one of several benefits linked to the Mediterranean diet, which is heavy in fish, vegetables, and olive oil.

Diets in areas with a high prevalence of a certain ailment tend to make use of locally sourced foodstuffs with a reputation for healing. Ingredients that have a long history of use in both cooking and medicine include spices like turmeric in South Asia and cactus in Mexico.

In summary:

The fascinating history, customs, and adaptive methods of many civilizations around the world are reflected in the impact of geographical and climatic factors on food choices. From coastal coastlines to barren deserts, from lush plains to frigid tundras, the natural landscapes we occupy have a profound impact on the foods we eat.

Indulging in the diverse cuisines of the world reveals a narrative with every bite—one of ingenuity, adaptation, and the profound bond between people and their natural surroundings. Food choices are a reflection of the ever-changing relationship between humans and the environment, impacted by factors such as the availability of certain crops, the effects of weather on taste, and innovative responses to difficult circumstances.

Reflection on the interconnectedness of global culinary traditions.

Connecting people across decades, regions, and cultures, culinary traditions are like threads in a fabric of human history. Nowadays, everyone lives in an interdependent global village, and the food industry is a prime example of this. Global culinary traditions are intricately linked through the blending of flavors, the sharing of culinary methods across cultures, and the mutual admiration for varied cuisines. In this introspection, we look at how food can bring people together, regardless of their nationality, and help them feel more connected to one another.

The Crossroads of Cuisine:

No exploration of world cuisines would be complete without stopping at the points where different civilizations meet. People from all over the globe have been in close proximity to one another throughout history due to migrations, conquests, and trade routes, and as a result, there has been a rich interchange of culinary traditions. For example, the Silk Road became a medium for the transfer of culinary traditions, herbs, spices, and other culinary arts from the East to the West, in addition to the trade of products.

Recent epochs have seen an acceleration in gastronomic heritage blending as a result of human mobility, be it immigration, tourism, or globalization. The culinary scenes of today's cities are a reflection of the cultural melting pots that have recently formed in these urban centers. In the process, classic meals undergo exciting flavor fusions, giving rise to whole new culinary landscapes.

An International Perspective on Ingredients:

The worldwide distribution of ingredients is one of the most obvious ways in which different cuisines around the world are interdependent. Supermarkets and grocery stores worldwide now stock ingredients from all over the globe, which were before thought to be unique and exclusive to certain regions. Because of this accessibility, people's cooking methods have been transformed, and the range of culinary possibilities has been expanded.

Just think of the avocado: it used to be an essential ingredient in many South and Central American dishes. These days, you may find it in sweets, salads, and sandwiches all around the globe. In a similar vein, South Asian spices such as turmeric, coriander, and cumin have made their way into kitchens all over the world, where they enhance the flavor and aroma of countless foods.

The enhanced flavors of local cuisines are a result of the globalization of ingredients, which also opens the door to creative improvisation. Everywhere you look, there's a global pantry full of ingredients that chefs and home cooks can use to create dishes that are truly unique and delicious.

Fusion Food as a Universal Language of Taste:

The rise of fusion cuisine is evidence of how different cuisines around the world are interdependent. It is an artistic representation of how different tastes and methods can combine to make something fresh and fascinating. As a culinary language that reflects the dynamic character of our linked globe, fusion food goes beyond regional boundaries.

Korean tacos combine the flavor of Korean BBQ with the convenience of Mexican street food, and they are popular in multicultural places like Los Angeles. Similarly, you may get Indian-inspired pizzas and Japanese-Peruvian ceviche on the London restaurant scene. Not only do these hybrid dishes honor the seamless blending of tastes from all around the globe, but they also mirror the multiethnic character of these cities.

Some think that fusion food waters down traditional dishes too much, and they aren't the only ones who feel this way. On the other hand, those who support it see it as a tribute to variety, a method to preserve cultural traditions in the kitchen while still catering to modern, multicultural palates.

The Impact of Migration on the Culinary Arts:

One of the most influential factors in the development of the ties between different cuisines around the world is migration. Not only do people take their possessions with them when they cross borders, but they also bring their culturally specific cooking methods, recipes, and dietary preferences. In many places of the world, ethnic enclaves have flourished as a result of the transfer of culinary knowledge.

Migrants' culinary traditions are still very much alive and well in ethnic districts like Little Italy, Chinatown, and others. Traditional foods are cooked with a degree of authenticity that brings the flavors of the country to life in these communities. In addition, these culinary traditions frequently spread throughout society, impacting local cuisine and fostering an interchange of culinary techniques across different cultures.

As an example, a culinary sensation began in the United States in the mid-20th century when Japanese immigrants brought sushi. Nowadays, sushi is adored all over the world, from Tokyo to New York to São Paulo, and is not just a popular Japanese meal.

Common Practices and Occasions:

Shared rituals and festivities highlight the linkages of culinary traditions around the world. Sharing a meal with loved ones is a universal human experience, regardless of cultural norms or cuisine. The significance of communal meals knows no borders; it is a staple of many celebrations around the world, from American Thanksgiving to Chinese New Year to the Middle Eastern iftar during Ramadan.

Both the variety of world cuisines and the universality of human experiences are brought to light by these shared rituals. The pleasure of sharing a meal, the wisdom of cooking together, and the customs of many cultures all weave together to form a diverse and interdependent culinary tapestry on a global scale.

Honoring Pasture-Based Traditions:

There is a rising understanding of the significance of conserving culinary legacy, even as new and interesting flavors have evolved as a result of the linkages of global culinary traditions. The authenticity of traditional foods and the stories they convey are being more valued as a response to the fast pace of globalization.

Documenting ancient recipes, supporting local farmers and producers, and promoting sustainable and ethical food practices are all ways to keep culinary history safe. All of these efforts are directed toward making sure that when different cuisines from across the world come together, it's not just about mixing and matching ingredients; it's also about preserving the cultural heritage that makes each dish special.

In summary:

It is evident that food is a potent force that goes beyond boundaries and languages when one considers the interdependencies of culinary traditions around the world. A universal dialogue about our common humanity emerges via the mingling of tastes, the exchange of recipes, and the enjoyment of varied culinary traditions. Everyone, from the crowded marketplaces of Marrakech to the street vendors of Bangkok, from the trattorias of Rome to the mobile restaurants of Mexico City, shares a passion for delicious cuisine and the stories it conveys.

Maintaining an attitude of wonder, reverence, and gratitude is crucial as we make our way across this intricate gastronomic terrain. Every dish adds to the story of world cuisine, whether it's based on ancient recipes or the result of modern fusions. By celebrating the shared roots of cuisines around the world, we can break down barriers of language and culture and bring people together around a common table where everyone may feel at home.

How farming practices influence the flavor and quality of ingredients

In this gastronomic adventure, the subtleties of farming techniques are the defining characteristics of the path from farm to table. The origins of the tastes, textures, and attributes that characterize food can be traced back to farms, which are more than just sources of raw ingredients. This essay delves into the complex relationships between farming and the culinary arts by investigating how farming techniques affect the flavor and quality of food.

The Foundation of the Soil:

The soil is the unsung hero of the culinary world, but it is also the bedrock of agricultural techniques. The flavor profile of crops is built upon the makeup of the soil, which is rich in minerals, organic materials, and microbes. Although generally linked with wine, the idea of terroir—the impact of soil on flavor—applies to a wide range of agricultural goods.

The tomatoes from Sicily, for example, have a distinct flavor that comes from the volcanic soils that grow there. The soil's minerals give tomatoes their unique flavor, turning them into a regional specialty rather than just an ingredient. To keep and improve ingredient quality, it is crucial to understand soil health and to cultivate it through sustainable strategies like cover cropping and crop rotation.

Climate and Terroir: A Ballet in Motion:

The weather, another instrument in the agricultural symphony, has a major impact on the taste and quality of the products. Crop development and maturity are influenced by the dynamic relationship between precipitation, temperature, and sunshine. Wines made from grapes cultivated in warmer parts of California, for instance, will have different flavors and aromas than those from cooler parts of Burgundy, France.

In a similar vein, the growing altitude has a significant impact on the final flavor of coffee beans. Beans grown at higher altitudes tend to have a more nuanced and complex flavor profile because of the cooler temperatures and slower maturation. The climate and elevation of the coffee's growing region, or "terroir," is a major component in establishing the bean's quality and marketability.

A Unique Beginning:

Even the seeds themselves are part of farming techniques, which go beyond only weather and soil. The ultimate harvest's flavor and quality are heavily dependent on the seeds used, which are in turn affected by variables including genetic diversity and adaptation to local conditions. For example, in the pursuit of uniformity in contemporary agriculture, heritage or heirloom varieties are sometimes overlooked, despite their highly valued distinctive flavors and traits.

The unique sparkling wines of Champagne, France are made on vineyards that prioritize the use of Pinot Noir, Chardonnay, and Pinot Meunier grape varieties, all of which contribute to the region's commitment to winemaking excellence. Similarly, farmers that continue to grow traditional tomato, apple, or grain types help ensure that some flavors will endure even in the face of competition from more commercially popular, mass-produced kinds.

Flavor Cultivation in Agriculture:

Particular agricultural techniques have a direct impact on flavor development, in addition to the intrinsic traits of soil, weather, and seeds. For example, organic farming typically yields more robust and unadulterated product since it prioritizes natural pest management methods and avoids synthetic chemicals. Aromas and flavors are more nuanced because of the focus on biodiversity in organic systems.

Regenerative farming strategies have an impact on flavor as well. These practices aim to restore and improve the ecosystem's health. Creating an environment where crops thrive organically is the goal of regenerative agriculture, which prioritizes soil health, carbon sequestration, and water conservation. In addition to improving flavors, this all-encompassing method may help agricultural systems become more resilient and sustainable.

How Agricultural Methods Affect the Environment:

The methods used for growing these ingredients have a significant impact on their final quality and taste. In the realm of tea, for instance, the way the leaves are picked and processed determines the quality of the finished product. The flavor characteristics of teas harvested by machine and those harvested by hand can differ. Green, black, and oolong teas all have unique flavors that originate from the oxidation and fermentation procedures used to make them.

In the world of viticulture, the concentration of flavor in wine is affected by the pruning, training, and management of grapevines. Flavors in wine grapes are developed by a number of factors, including the ratio of leaf cover to fruit exposure, the timing of harvest, and irrigation techniques.

When and how ripe to harvest:

When items are picked at the optimal time determines how good they taste. At its most flavorful and nutritious, every crop has a certain ripening window. Flavor is typically sacrificed for uniformity and shelf life in modern industrial agriculture, which prioritizes fixed harvest timings for logistical convenience.

On the other hand, a more sophisticated strategy may appeal to small-scale or artisanal producers whose focus is on taste rather than product longevity. The sugars, acids, and volatile chemicals that give fruits and vegetables their flavor are at their peak when picked at the exact moment they achieve peak ripeness.

Operations Following Harvest:

The quality of ingredients might be further affected by their handling after harvest. The key to flavor preservation is careful temperature control, proper storage, and processing after harvest. Because of their fragility, herbs and leafy greens, for instance, must be handled with extreme care and cooled quickly to retain their flavor and freshness.

Drying and roasting are two examples of the post-harvest processing procedures that have a major influence on the flavor characteristic of coffee. Coffees with nutty, chocolatey, fruity, or flowery notes can be made from the same beans by employing different processing methods.

Getting There and Being Close to Customers:

Another factor that might affect the taste and quality of ingredients is the distance that they travel from the farm to the market. In many cases, the freshness and flavor of locally obtained produce outshines that of products that have traveled great distances. As a result, there is a fresh push to lessen the environmental impact of food transportation and to back local farmers.

The significance of reducing the length of the supply chain has been brought to light by the rise of farm-to-table movements, farmers' markets, and community-supported agriculture (CSA) programs. These methods help local economies thrive while also keeping products' nutrients and flavors intact by bringing buyers in close contact with farmers.

Farming and Customer Preferences:

Consumer tastes and needs are just one more way in which agricultural methods affect flavor. More and more people are starting to pay attention to the effects of agriculture on our health and the environment, and they are looking for flavors that represent sustainable and regenerative farming methods. Organic, biodynamic, or locally sourced products are becoming more and more sought after by consumers who want to support businesses that share their beliefs.

The changing tastes of consumers impact farming methods in turn. To meet the need for sustainable and high-quality produce, farmers are turning to agroecological practices, which put an emphasis on soil health and encourage the exploration of traditional or heirloom crop types with unique characteristics.

In summary:

Farming methods take center stage as dancers in the complex interplay between the land and the plate, molding the taste and excellence of the components. Every aspect of farming, from the soil's embrace to the cultivation techniques used, from seed selection to harvest timing, adds to the gastronomic symphony that plays out in kitchens all around the globe.

Thinking about how agricultural techniques affect flavor makes it obvious that farm decisions affect the whole food system. Every item has a story—the terroir-driven Bordeaux wines, the heirloom tomatoes from the farmers' market, the coffee beans from a small cooperative that are sourced responsibly. The stories are written in the fields by the people who tend to the land.

We can all have a role in creating the flavors of tomorrow by being aware of how our food choices affect the agricultural landscape. We can help create a story in the food industry that celebrates the interdependence of the farm, the plate, and the bright flavors that turn every meal into an ode to the land's bounty by backing farming practices that put an emphasis on flavor, sustainability, and environmental health.

Exploring the importance of soil health and seed selection in agriculture.

The soil is the bedrock of fertile harvests in the great agricultural landscapes. Concurrently, the seeds planted in this soil have the potential to yield harvests in the future. The foundation of sustainable and productive agriculture is the symbiotic interaction between seed selection and soil health. Soil health and seed selection are the focus of this investigation because of the significant roles they play in agricultural systems' resilience, nutritional content, and crop output.

Soil Health as the Foundation of Agriculture: The Living Earth

The soil is more than just a plant-holding medium; it is a vibrant ecosystem rich with bacteria, fungus, and innumerable other creatures that all work together to keep the soil healthy. In order to foster plant growth, soil quality is determined by a complex interplay of physical, chemical, and biological factors.

In terms of its physical health, soil is primarily defined by its structure and texture. The bigger particles in sandy soils provide for adequate drainage, although the soil may be deficient in nutrients. Although they are able to hold water, compacted clayey soils have smaller particles. Many farmers believe that loamy soils, which are a balanced blend, are the best for growing crops. Plant development is influenced by the soil's physical structure in three ways: root penetration, water retention, and aeration.

Chemical Features: Nutrient Availability is Highly Influenced by Soil Chemistry. The nutrient density of crops is enhanced by micronutrients and essential elements such as potassium, nitrogen, and phosphorus. Soil pH affects nutrient solubility, which in turn affects plant uptake of those nutrients. Soil nutrient management relies on an understanding of and adherence to soil chemistry.

Biological Characteristics: Nematodes, fungus, and bacteria all coexist in soil. These creatures work as symbiotic partners with plants, break down organic materials, and contribute to nutrient cycling. Soil fertility, nutrient availability, and disease suppression are all impacted by a balanced soil biome.

Soil Management: A Master Class in Art and Science

It is necessary to take a comprehensive approach to soil management in order to achieve and sustain soil health. A healthy soil ecosystem is crucial to agricultural output in the long run, which is why sustainable farming methods center on maintaining and improving soil health. Soil management entails, among other things:

Planting cover crops in the winter or spring helps keep soil from washing away, increases organic matter, and boosts biodiversity. You can reduce your reliance on synthetic fertilizers by growing cover crops like legumes, which fix nitrogen in the soil.

Optimal nutrient use, reduced disease pressure, and broken pest cycles are all results of careful crop rotation. Crop rotation is useful for maintaining a steady soil fertility level since different crops have different nutritional needs.

Compost and manure are examples of organic materials that can improve soil structure, water retention, and nutrient availability. Soil microbes thrive on organic matter, which in turn supports a rich and varied soil environment.

Less Tillage: Tilling the soil too much will break down organic matter and soil structure. Soil structure, erosion, and carbon sequestration are all improved by reduced tillage or no-till farming techniques.

Conservation Methods: Terracing and contour plowing are two examples of conservation methods that can reduce the likelihood of soil erosion. Soil health, nutrient retention, and agricultural landscape integrity are all greatly enhanced by effective erosion control measures.

How to Choose Seeds for a Successful Harvest

When it comes to agricultural productivity, soil health is like a canvas; the seeds you choose are like the brushstrokes that determine the ultimate artwork. Selecting seed variants that are well-suited to a particular ecosystem is an intricate art form. Varieties of seeds differ in their genetic composition, which impacts characteristics like insect resistance, suitability to particular temperatures, and productivity.

The success rate of a crop is directly proportional to how well its seeds adapt to the local climate. Seeds that are resistant to climate change can endure changes in water supply, temperature, and other environmental factors. In dry areas, for instance, seeds that can withstand low water levels are essential for a steady crop.

Pest and Disease Resistance: To lessen the need for chemical interventions, it is possible to select seeds that are naturally resistant to common pests and diseases. By reducing the negative effects of agriculture on the environment without sacrificing crop health, this method is in line with sustainable agricultural principles.

Seed genetics have a direct impact on the nutritional value of crops. Food security and issues surrounding malnutrition can be addressed through the use of seeds developed for increased nutritional content. In areas where certain nutritional deficits are common, this is of paramount importance.

Seeds with a high yield potential are generally sought after by farmers who want to maximize productivity. There should be a balance between yield and other considerations, like efficient use of resources and environmental sustainability. The ideal traits for high-yielding cultivars include resilience and adaptability.

Advancements in Seed Science

The advent of precision agriculture, made possible by technological advancements in seed production, has provided farmers with a wide range of seed varieties tailored to address certain issues. Here are a few noteworthy advancements:

Biotechnology and Genetic Modification (GM): GM includes inserting certain genes into a plant's DNA to give it desirable characteristics, such pest resistance or herbicide tolerance. While genetically modified (GM) crops have found widespread use in some areas, others worry about their effects on the environment and the safety of the food they eat.

Targeted alterations to a plant's genome are made possible using precision breeding techniques, such as CRISPR-Cas9 gene editing. New seed types with desired features can be developed more precisely and under more controlled conditions using these procedures.

The purpose of biofortified seeds is to increase the nutrient density of the final crop. One example is biofortified rice, which increases the quantities of beta-carotene, a provitamin A, in the grains in an effort to combat vitamin A insufficiency.

Seed Choosing and Soil Health: Some Considerations and Obstacles

Even if farmers have access to useful tools thanks to advances in seed technology, there are still certain things to think about and handle:

Worries about Biodiversity: A decline in crop diversity may result from the dominance of a small number of high-yielding varieties. It is possible that agricultural systems become more susceptible to pests and illnesses when they practice monocultures, or the widespread cultivation of a single crop.

Modern seed varieties are typically dependent on synthetic fertilizers and pesticides since they are bred to operate optimally under specified conditions. The long-term viability of agricultural systems and the effects on the environment are questions that this reliance brings up.

Equity and Access: Small-scale and resource-limited farmers may face difficulties in gaining access to new seeds and technologies. For agriculture to be inclusive and sustainable, it is crucial that everyone has access to high-quality seeds and that traditional seed-saving methods are supported.

The manufacturing of seeds, particularly genetically modified (GM) and hybrid seeds, can have an effect on the environment. The seed industry must implement sustainable practices because the production and distribution of seeds add to agriculture's carbon footprint.

Moving Forward in Harmony: How to Choose Seeds While Ensuring Soil Health

A resilient and sustainable agricultural system can only be fostered by acknowledging the interdependence of seed selection and soil health. When bringing these two crucial parts together, keep these guidelines in mind:

The ever-changing nature of our natural surroundings is recognized through the adoption of adaptive agriculture practices. System resilience and sustainability are enhanced when farmers adjust seed selection in response to changing weather patterns and soil quality in their respective regions.

Agroecology: Agroecological methods place an emphasis on farming practices that are in harmony with nature. Agroecology improves soil health and decreases reliance on external inputs by imitating natural processes like pest regulation and nutrient cycle.

Preservation of Crop Biodiversity and Improvement of Local Adaptation are Two Outcomes of Farm-Storage-Related Seed Saving and Exchange Programs. For the most part, seeds that have been kept from farms are ideal for growing in a particular area.

The only way to deal with new problems and take advantage of new opportunities is to keep researching soil science and seed technology. Agriculture as a whole is more resilient thanks to innovations that put an emphasis on biodiversity, farmer autonomy, and environmental sustainability.

Education and Extension: Enabling farmers to make educated decisions requires providing them with knowledge about soil health management and seed selection. In order to spread best practices and encourage the adoption of sustainable alternatives, extension services are vital.

In sum: laying the Groundwork for Long-Term Sustainability in Agriculture

The importance of healthy soil and careful seed selection is becoming more obvious as we traverse the complicated landscape of contemporary agriculture. Agricultural systems rely on these factors as their foundation for resilience and productivity. The intricate web of life in the agricultural process extends from the subterranean realm of soil microbes to the genetic code contained within seeds.

A comprehensive strategy that acknowledges the complex interplay between soil health and seed selection is necessary for the advancement of sustainable agriculture. The future of agriculture is shaped by a diverse group of people, including farmers, academics, lawmakers, and consumers. Sustainable and prosperous agricultural ecosystems are born from practices that prioritize soil health, biodiversity conservation, and equal access to excellent seeds. May the seeds of transformation we plant take hold in rich, verdant soil, where they can flourish and bear fruit that will nourish the earth and its caretakers for years to come.

How farming practices influence the flavor and quality of ingredients.

Nature and nurture are inseparable; the ingredients we consume aren't just a lucky break; they're the product of a balanced partnership between farmers' labor and the land's vitality. Farming techniques conduct a culinary symphony from seed to plate, with each step adding to the ultimate flavor and texture composition. This investigation elucidates the scientific and artistic processes that go into producing the food we love by exposing the huge impact of farming methods on ingredient quality and flavor.

Nurturing the Foundation: A Symphony of Soil

The earth is the foundation of farming; it is a living, breathing thing that holds the very soul of farming in its embrace. Soil quality and composition are foundational elements impacting crop flavor and quality. The idea of terroir, which is commonly linked with wine, goes beyond the vineyards to highlight how a particular geographical area influences the flavor of food.

Crop nutrition and taste are affected by the complex interplay of soil nutrients such as nitrogen, phosphorus, potassium, and countless micronutrients. Complex flavors are enhanced by soils that are well-balanced, but dull flavor and poor quality can be the outcome of nutrient shortages or imbalances.

Underneath the surface, a thriving microbial life forms a symbiotic bond with plants. Plants' ability to absorb nutrients, resist diseases, and stay healthy is aided by mycorrhizal fungi, bacteria, and other soil-dwelling creatures. The terroir, which in turn shapes the unique tastes of crops, is affected by the variety and quantity of these microbes.

Conscious farming techniques maintain soil health, which in turn promotes sustainability. Organic matter incorporation, crop rotation, and cover crops all work together to improve soil structure, water retention, and microbial activity. Not only can sustainable soil techniques improve flavor, they also help the agricultural ecosystem be more resilient in the long run.

Planting the Right Varieties for Success: Seeds of Legacy

Every adventure starts with a seed, a little receptacle with the DNA code for the plant it will grow into. Farmers must carefully consider which seed kinds to use because these choices affect not just the yield but also the quality, taste, and texture of the final product.

The renaissance of traditional and antique seed kinds is evidence of the value placed on their distinct aromas, tastes, and textures. These seeds, which are typically passed down through families, help keep biodiversity alive and provide a wide range of flavors that might otherwise be lost in the quest for standardization.

Climate Adaptation: For optimal agricultural yields, it is crucial to choose seed kinds that are well-suited to the local climate. Producing crops with ideal flavor and quality is more probable when seeds are cultivated in settings that are ideal for them in terms of temperature, humidity, and day length. The adaptability of agricultural systems to shifting weather patterns is enhanced by the use of climate-adapted cultivars.

Modern farmers use genetic modification to provide their crops better defenses against pests or more resilience to drought. Increased yield and decreased pesticide use are two advantages of this technique, but how it will affect flavor and quality is still up for debate and investigation.

A Tasteful Approach to Agriculture: Taking Care of the Harvest

The cultivation procedures that farmers apply after sowing the seeds greatly influence the quality and taste of the harvest. Every choice—from watering schedules to pest control—affects the crops' ultimate personality.

The formation of flavor relies on the careful management of water. Controlled irrigation can improve the sweetness and avoid bitterness in some crops, while well-drained soil is ideal for others. Sustainable water management strategies help bring out the best flavors while also preserving a valuable resource.

Knowing when to harvest is a skill that only the most seasoned farmers have mastered. Harvest timing affects crop ripeness, which in turn affects texture, sweetness, and flavor. The ingredients' quality might be affected if harvesting is done at the wrong time of day.

Integrated Pest Management (IPM): Strategic pest management is essential for maintaining a delicate farm ecosystem. Natural predators, crop rotation, and targeted pesticide use are all part of an integrated pest management strategy. By using this method, we can protect the environment while still enjoying the authentic flavors of our crops.

The growing popularity of biodynamic and organic farming methods shows a desire to grow food without harming the environment. Organic inputs, cover crops, and holistic farm management replace synthetic chemicals in these methods. The end product usually has a stronger, more genuine taste because of it.

Preservation of the Essence through Post-Harvest Handling

The post-harvest handling of the crops is crucial for preserving and improving their quality and flavor. Every stage of the post-harvest process, from shipping to storage, is a fine waltz that can bring out or hide the true flavors of the components.

To keep perishable goods tasting their best, it is crucial to manage the cold chain from farm to market in a consistent manner. The volatile chemicals that give food its flavor and scent degrade more slowly in controlled environments.

Minimal Processing: By minimizing processing, the essential flavors of crops are preserved. Gentle washing and pruning is beneficial for some crops, but overprocessing herbs, for example, can strip them of their flavor and vital oils. A growing demand for foods with natural, unprocessed flavors is congruent with the current trend toward less processed options.

Using Local Sources: The amount of time an ingredient spends in transit from farm to fork has a direct effect on its flavor. The full range of flavors is generally preserved in locally sourced produce since it reaches consumers when it is at its freshest. Local sourcing has becoming more important as people want to know more about the farms that provide the food they eat.

Climate as a Fingerprint on the Environment

Even while farmers can only do so much to influence the quality and taste of their ingredients, external factors like climate and weather patterns have a profound impact. Weather events such as droughts, excessive heat, or unusual precipitation can affect the flavor and visual appeal of harvested foods.

Climate Variability: Flavor profiles can vary due to changes in weather patterns and temperature fluctuations. Wines made from grapes cultivated during a cooler season, for instance, could have more acidity and unique aromatic traits. Farmers who want their crops to have a consistent flavor face both threats and opportunities from the climate's unpredictability.

The idea of terroir is highly esteemed in wine-producing regions. This is because locals there understand that each grape's flavor is a product of its specific soil, climate, and location. This idea is gaining popularity in other agricultural settings as a way to honor the complex tastes that result from the interaction of different environmental elements.

A Gastronomic Collaboration: The Craftsmanship of Farmers

Fundamentally, farming is an art form, requiring a mutually beneficial relationship between farmers and the land they tend. Every step of the growing process, from tilling the soil to choosing the seeds, from planting the seeds to tending to them after harvest, is an artistic endeavor that impacts the flavor of the food that people eat.

The cultural importance and distinctive flavor of many traditional and heirloom varieties contribute to their high value in preserving culinary heritage. The farmers who work to maintain and spread these varieties are weaving a tapestry of culinary history that will allow people of all ages to enjoy the tastes of yesteryear.

Responsible Land Stewardship: The movement towards sustainable and regenerative farming practices demonstrates farmers' dedication to responsible land stewardship. Improved crop flavor and a more robust and long-term food system are both outcomes of farmers' efforts to promote soil health, biodiversity, and ecological balance.

Connections from Farm to Table: The "farm-to-table" movement highlights the importance of the one-on-one interaction between farmers and their customers. Reduced time spent in transit and storage means that customers may enjoy ingredients at their best quality, thanks to a shorter supply chain.

A Culinary Connoisseurship: The Role of the Consumer

Our purchasing habits influence agricultural methods and, by extension, the food we eat. By delving into the complexities of how farming techniques impact flavor, we can make well-informed decisions that reflect our values and preferences.

In Support of Sustainable Practices: You can help keep the planet healthy and taste true by buying from farmers that use sustainable and regenerative methods. People may do their part to promote sustainability in the food industry by shopping locally, prioritizing organic products, and thinking about how their food choices affect the environment.

We may expand our culinary horizons by embracing the numerous flavors that result from different farming practices and regional terroirs. You can experience a wide range of flavors through farmer's markets, CSA programs, and developing personal relationships with farmers.

When we, the customers, speak out about how important it is that food tastes good and is of high quality, we help shape the priorities of the food sector. A change towards agricultural methods that place an emphasis on flavor, among other things, is being driven by the need for high-quality, tasty ingredients.

Summary: A Delicate Web of Flavors Crafted by Farmers' Hands

The tastes and excellence of ingredients are like threads spun by farmers' hands in the vast fabric of cuisine. Every choice made on the farm has an impact on the food that is cooked in kitchens all over the world, from the quality of the soil to the seeds used, from the methods of cultivation to the care taken with the produce after harvest.

By delving into the topic of how farming techniques impact flavor, we can forge a stronger bond with the source of our food. Indulging in the nuances of a hand-harvested tea or a vine-ripened tomato transports us to a world where the story of food goes much beyond the plate.

The farmers whose hard work and skill make these delicacies possible deserve our gratitude and support, and we have a responsibility as consumers, cooks, and activists to do more than just savor them. Together, we can create a culinary environment that honors the skill of farmers, who are both masters of their land and masters of flavor, by promoting sustainable practices, protecting culinary traditions, and savoring the variety of terroirs.

Personal stories of individuals who found passion and purpose in the kitchen.

Kitchens are more than just places to cook; they are also places where lives are shaped by the people who live there, the tales they tell, the memories they make, and, for some, the beginning of a deep quest for meaning and fulfillment. In this anthology of personal stories, we explore the lives of people who found a strong sense of purpose and a love for cooking in the kitchen. The stories showcase the life-altering potential of culinary arts, showing how something as mundane as cooking can lead to profound introspection and happiness.

My Journey from Engineer to Chef: A Culinary Odyssey

Introducing Sarah, a life-altering event who found her niche in the kitchen after pursuing a career in engineering. Sarah signed up for a cooking class completely by accident after becoming bored with her desk job. She had no idea that her tentative forays into the culinary arts would pave the way for a life-altering experience. Eventually, the kitchen evolved from a pastime into a lifelong calling.

Sarah refined her abilities through culinary school and an apprenticeship program, where she learned how to use knives expertly, create mouth-watering taste combinations, and achieve the precise balance that elevates any meal to a gourmet level. She found solace and inspiration in the kitchen, which had previously been a frightening area. Sarah is now the proud owner of her own catering business, where she uses her exceptional culinary skills and meticulous engineering skills to create one-of-a-kind dishes.

A Recovery Journey through Cooking

The therapeutic act of cooking had a significant role in John's recovery and resilience. As John sought solace in the kitchen following a horrific incident, he began to heal on a personal level. A potent instrument for emotional healing emerged from what started as a harmless pastime.

For John, tinkering with different components and recipes was like meditating; it gave him a sense of mastery and achievement. As he worked through the intricacies of recovery, he realized that the magic of the kitchen could restore not just damaged recipes, but also pieces of his own identity. John continues to transform the kitchen into a haven for healing and connection by sharing his culinary creations with others who are also on the road to recovery.

A Journey in Culinary Activism: From Chef to Advocate for Food Justice

Maria discovered her calling in the fast-paced world of professional kitchens by applying her talents to solve larger social problems through the creation of mouth-watering meals. She saw firsthand the problems of food waste, injustice, and producer-consumer divide while working in well-known restaurants. Maria left her career as a chef to pursue food justice because she was so driven to make a positive impact.

She promotes a more just food system, helps local farmers thrive, and informs people about sustainable eating through her initiatives. Maria sees the kitchen as more than simply a space for cooking; it's also a chance to make a difference in people's lives. Her incredible journey exemplifies how a deep love for food, coupled with a determination to tackle larger social issues, may bring about profound change.

A Chef's Role in Developing Future Chefs

Michael discovered his life's work in the culinary arts education, where he gets to mold the careers of future chefs. His grandma started him on his culinary journey by teaching him the family dishes in a little kitchen. Michael followed his passion for teaching others how to cook by combining the best of traditional and contemporary methods, driven by his love of passing on his skills to others.

Michael learned in class that the kitchen is a great setting for many things, including honing one's culinary abilities, exploring one's creative side, and developing an appreciation for the rich history and variety of food cultures around the world. His students not only become excellent cooks, but they also learn a great deal about the background and significance of the food they prepare. Michael uses the kitchen as a classroom, teaching students not only how to cook but also how to love learning new things.

The Path from Home Chef to Food Industry Behemoth: Culinary Entrepreneurship

As a prime example of how one's enthusiasm and drive may take them from being an enthusiastic home cook to a prosperous food industry entrepreneur, consider Anna's story. Making elaborate desserts and tinkering with different flavors as a pastime turned into a successful career. Before it became the core of her entrepreneurial aspirations, the kitchen was a private place for Anna to experiment with her food.

Anna turned her passion for baking into a thriving business by deftly navigating the ins and outs of food startup, from finding high-quality ingredients to advertising her products. Her tale encourages would-be entrepreneurs to follow their passions and make a living doing what they love, and her items are now sold in local stores.

Conclusion: The Flavorful Web of Individual Stories

These anecdotes show how different people discover their calling in the kitchen. Stories abound in the culinary arts, from those who transitioned from corporate America to the culinary arts, from those who found solace in the kitchen during times of hardship, from those who used their skills to effect social change, from those who inspired the next generation of chefs to those who turned their home cooking hobby into a successful business.

The rhythmic jingling of knives on cutting boards, the perfume of spices, and the sound of boiling pans transform the kitchen into more than just a place to cook. It becomes a haven for people to come and learn about themselves, recover, become activists, educate, and start their own businesses. Transcending the confines of the kitchen and touching on the common human experience of discovering one's passion, these personal narratives encourage us to recognize the immense influence that cooking can have on a person's life.

How cooking becomes a form of self-expression and creativity.

The kitchen may become a haven from the hectic pace of daily life, a place where regular chores can be turned into a remarkable canvas for artistic expression. As a medium for the expression of feelings, cultural heritage, and personal stories, cooking takes on a life of its own beyond that of a simple means of subsistence. As we delve into this topic, we uncover the complex web of ways in which cooking influences not only the food but also the cook's sense of self.

Creating Flavor Symphonies: An Auditory Extravaganza

The art of cooking is in the careful blending of flavors, which create a mesmerizing symphony of smells, tastes, and textures. A chef's ingredient selection is like a conductor's symphony; they must strike a delicate balance between sweet and savory, between different textures, and between complex scents.

Envision a chef enhancing a plain tomato sauce with a touch of balsamic vinegar, garlic, and basil. The culinary score is like a musical score, with each ingredient playing a part in the dish's overall melody. Cooking is like conducting an orchestra; the conductor adjusts the timing and seasoning to achieve a harmonious blend that reflects their particular style and tastes as much as it does the palate.

Broad Brushstrokes: The Identity and Heritage of Culinary Arts

Many people's cultural identities and heritages are expressed via their culinary practices. The cook's identity is shaped by the different cultural influences they encounter, which are revealed through traditional culinary techniques, recipes passed down through generations, and the items they choose to use.

Envision a modern take on a traditional recipe that incorporates elements from the chef's cultural heritage. A chef's ability to pay homage to their cultural heritage while also showcasing the diverse array of world cuisines is a powerful statement when they skillfully combine classic ingredients with contemporary techniques. In this setting, the act of cooking itself becomes a cultural discussion, a way to honor heritage while welcoming new ideas.

The Art of Improvisation: Unleashing Your Creativity in the Kitchen

When cooking, spontaneity is key, and chefs transform into improvising performers. There are many reasons why cooks stray from recipes and embrace the freedom to improvise. It could be because of what's in the cupboard, what's in season, or a spontaneous flash of inspiration.

Just picture a home cook going a little bit wild with different spices, playing about with different amounts, and switching things up depending on what they like. In a kitchen that encourages innovation, slip-ups are seen as learning experiences rather than setbacks. Improvisation allows the chef more leeway to express themselves creatively and personally throughout the cooking process.

The Art of Visual Art: Shifting from the Kitchen to the Canvas

As plating becomes an art form in and of itself, the creative representation of a meal goes beyond just its flavor. When plating food, both professional chefs and amateurs pay close attention to form, color, and texture. The end product is more than simply food; it's an aesthetic masterpiece that tempts the senses even before consumption.

Imagine a chef expertly plating a dish with artfully dripping a reduction over perfectly cooked protein while carefully positioning colorful vegetables on top. As the chef uses spatulas and tweezers, the plate transforms into a work of art. The history of the ingredients, the chef's creative process, and the dish's presentation all come together on each plate.

Poems for the Seasons: How the Landscape Affects the Food We Eat

As the seasons change, so does the variety of foods that are available, giving food a poetic quality that is uniquely its own. The chef, in sync with the natural world's tempo, transforms into a poet as he or she creates seasonal delicacies. When spring rolls around, you could find yourself craving light, airy salads and delicate herbs, while the cold, dark days of winter call for hearty stews and roasted root veggies.

Thus, the kitchen serves as a medium through which the ebb and flow of nature's moods are conveyed, and the chef, like a poet, transforms the splendor of the season's foodstuffs into gastronomic poetry. Choosing and preparing food that is in season is a way to show that you are in tune with nature.

Telling Tales in the Kitchen: Filling Tales on the Dish

A tale, just waiting to be told, resides within every dish. The chef transforms the kitchen into a storytelling platform by creating mouth-watering narratives out of disparate ingredients, techniques, and cultural influences. No matter if it's re-creating a family recipe or pulling inspiration from faraway places, the plate serves as a backdrop for stories told via food.

Envision a chef incorporating elements that bring back fond memories of a certain occasion or location into a dish. The chef takes on the role of storyteller, transporting the audience to another world as they savor every mouthful. The art of culinary storytelling has the dual benefit of satisfying the appetite and the spirit by forging an intimate bond among the chef, the food, and the audience.

The Therapeutic Art of Cooking: Promoting the Health and Happiness of the Chef

A lot of people find that cooking is a good way to release their emotions and take care of themselves. Aspirations are transformed into dough and anxieties are reduced to a pot of soothing soup in the kitchen, which serves as a sanctuary from the outside world. As the chef chops, stirs, and measures, he or she finds a meditative rhythm that brings them into the here and now.

Envision a frustrated baker releasing their pent-up energy into the repetitive actions of kneading bread. For many people, cooking is a therapeutic activity; when they let their emotions run wild in the kitchen, it shows in the food they make. Here, the act of cooking takes on the qualities of a therapeutic craft, helping one to relax and focus.

Breaking New Ground in the Kitchen: Questioning the Status Quo

Innovation is key when it comes to cooking as a creative pursuit. Both professional and amateur cooks with visionary minds are always pushing the envelope, changing the way food is prepared and what is considered possible in the kitchen. With each new invention, the kitchen becomes a veritable laboratory and the chef into an adventurous explorer of unexplored culinary realms.

Think of a chef trying out molecular gastronomy methods or a home cook adding new flavors to an old recipe. The kitchen is transformed into a whimsical haven for imaginative play, where delicacies are born that beyond all expectations. The innovative spirit of the cook and the dynamic nature of the culinary arts are both reflected in the dishes they create.

Final Thoughts: A Kitchen Canvas for Individual Expression

Cooking, like a magical enchantment, becomes an outlet for deep creative expression in the kitchen. The kitchen is a place where cooks express themselves through everything from creating flavor symphonies and weaving cultural narratives to performing impromptu dances and inventing new recipes.

Making food is more than just a chore; it's an art form that highlights uniqueness while bringing people together via shared sensory experiences. Indulging in the chef's lovingly crafted meals is like having a one-on-one chat with them; it's a discourse that goes beyond words and brings people together via the common language of food. Any dish prepared by a cook is like a work of art; each bite reveals a little bit of the artist's soul.

Exploring the evolving landscape of the culinary world.

Cultural, social, and technical changes are mirrored in the ever-evolving culinary world. The culinary environment is ever-changing, ranging from traditional kitchens that adhere to centuries-old methods to cutting-edge culinary laboratories that push the limits of creativity. In this investigation, we traverse the complex aspects of this dynamic environment, taking into account the effects of globalization, sustainability, culinary technology, and the shifting tastes of an eclectic and discriminating audience.

The Fusion of Globalization and Cuisine: A Variety of Flavors

The impact of globalization on the modern culinary scene is one of its most striking characteristics. A diverse tapestry of flavors, techniques, and ingredients is created when culinary traditions from all over the world come together. Fusion cuisines that chefs get their inspiration from a wide range of cultures allow customers to experience the flavors of the world in a single meal.

Picture yourself enjoying a meal that expertly combines French cooking techniques with Indian spices, or Latin American and Asian flavors. In today's ever-changing culinary scene, this fusion is celebrated and embraced, turning kitchens into multicultural nexuses where creativity has no limits.

The Conscious Farm-to-Table Movement in Sustainable Gastronomy

Sustainable practices are now integral to contemporary cuisine as people become more conscious of the need to protect our planet. Every step of the food chain, from production to consumption, is investigated for its impact on the environment. Sustainable practices that put an emphasis on ethical sourcing, waste reduction, and ecosystem health are sought after by both chefs and consumers.

Imagine a restaurant that highlights its relationships with local farmers that practice regenerative agriculture and publicly shows the provenance of its ingredients. There has been a shift toward a more conscientious approach to food as a result of the growing awareness of the link between sustainable agriculture and public health.

Technological Advancements in the Kitchen: A Revolution

The kitchen has entered a new era because to technological advancements that have changed the game for both professional chefs and amateurs alike. Technology has become an essential aspect of the culinary scene, allowing chefs to expand their creativity through the use of precision cooking gadgets and molecular gastronomy techniques.

Envision a chef who uses 3D printing to make elaborate food sculptures or sous-vide cooking to ensure exact temperature control. The boundaries between culinary art and science are becoming increasingly blurry as a result of technological advancements in the kitchen, which improve accuracy and efficiency while simultaneously opening up new possibilities for unparalleled creativity.

The Growing Number of Conscientious Consumers: Influencing Food Trends

The tastes of conscientious consumers are more important in the dynamic food industry. Modern customers are pickier than ever before, expecting restaurants to uphold higher standards of ethics, provide clear information about where their ingredients come from, and demonstrate a dedication to social responsibility in addition to serving delicious food.

Think about how much interest there is in plant-based options, which show that people are becoming more concerned about eating sustainably and healthily. Chefs and food companies are being pushed to adapt to new expectations and put an emphasis on ethical standards as they strive for culinary perfection by the growing trend of conscious consumption.

Empowering and Educating the Next Generation of Chefs through Culinary Arts

Culinary education and empowerment are also part of the culinary scene, which goes beyond professional kitchens. Many resources, like culinary schools and mentorship programs, are available to aspiring chefs today, allowing them to confront the many problems that the culinary industry always brings.

Imagine a student majoring in culinary arts who is also enrolled in a course that teaches them about sustainability, diversity in the kitchen, and business. In order to prepare students for a challenging and dynamic career in the food sector, culinary programs are adapting to meet the needs of the future.

The Culinary Spectacle and Its Popularity in the Food Industry

Nowadays, restaurants serve more than just meals; they're also a kind of entertainment. The growth of food-focused media, such as popular cookery shows and online food videos, has elevated the dining experience to the level of a sensory extravaganza. The kitchen has evolved into a dramatic and creative arena, and chefs and other culinary superstars have achieved superstar status.

Take a well-known cooking program as an example; the contestants compete not just on their culinary abilities but also on their storytelling and presenting skills. As an entertainment industry, the food industry has the ability to enthrall and motivate audiences, which in turn shapes public opinion and drives culinary trends.

Virtual Eating: Exploring the New Digital Landscape

Virtual eating experiences have emerged as a result of the expansion of digital technology into the realm of cuisine. As a result of worldwide crises like the COVID-19 epidemic, online platforms, meal delivery applications, and virtual cooking classes have become essential parts of the modern dining scene.

Envision yourself enrolled in a virtual cooking class where a world-class chef teaches you the tricks of their trade without ever having to leave your house. New opportunities for culinary discovery, education, and community involvement are opening up in the culinary world as it adapts to the digital frontier.

A Nod to the Past: Revisiting the Traditions of Food

In the culinary world, there is a trend toward going back to basics, which is happening simultaneously with the innovation and globalization wave. Traditional ingredients, methods, and recipes are being rediscovered and celebrated by both professional and amateur chefs. As it develops, the culinary landscape pays tribute to the traditional recipes and methods that give rise to the world's many cuisines.

Think of a restaurant whose chef is bringing back traditional preservation techniques or whose menu features dishes made with ancient grains. Recognizing the enduring wisdom in traditional methods, a return to culinary roots enriches the ever-expanding culinary world with depth and authenticity.

Final Thoughts: A Changing Culinary Scene

The ever-changing culinary scene is orchestrated by the harmonious sound of frying pans, fragrant spices, and inventive brains. It is a scene that has been molded by the coming together of varied and thoughtful audiences' preferences, environmental imperatives, technical advances, and worldwide influences.

We see the merging of tastes, the adoption of sustainability, the incorporation of technology, and the emancipation of both chefs and customers as we go across this culinary terrain. Since the culinary world is always changing, it mirrors not just the fads in food but also the shifting dynamics of our society.

Everything about the culinary world is a reflection of the times we live in—the deliberate choices of customers, the new techniques of chefs, the celebration of culinary heritage, and the digital revolutions in how we perceive food. As we move through this dynamic terrain, one thing is certain: the kitchen, with all its potential, will always be the meeting place of tradition, innovation, and invention in the realm of food.

Perspectives on innovation, sustainability, and the future of cooking

There is a magical chemistry taking place in the kitchen as sounds of clashing pots and blending flavors reshape the culinary landscape. With sustainability as our guiding philosophy, the future of cooking is unfolding before us as we stand at the intersection of tradition and innovation. This investigation dives into the many viewpoints of sustainability, innovation, and the fascinating future of cooking.

Reimagining Tradition via Innovation: Culinary Alchemy

Culinary innovation is like a chef's alchemy: taking ordinary ingredients and turning them into something magical. Modern chefs use the once-traditional kitchen as a testing ground for innovative dishes, techniques, and plating styles.

Imagine a chef who, with the help of molecular gastronomy, challenges the traditional textures of food by making foams, gels, and spheres. To innovate in this setting is not to abandon tradition but to give it a new meaning, to give old recipes and cooking methods a modern twist. Chefs who can expertly combine modern techniques with time-tested methods will be in demand in the years to come.

A Revolution in Food and Cooking: Sustainable Gastronomy

The concept of sustainability has become increasingly important in the food industry, changing the way professionals and amateurs alike think about food waste, where their food comes from, and how their dishes affect the environment. The focus on sustainability is changing the face of food from farm to fork.

Envision a restaurant that cut down on waste by using only locally sourced ingredients, embracing seasonal vegetables, and other eco-friendly practices. Sustainable gastronomy is more than a passing fad; it represents a sea change in our relationship with food. To make sure that enjoying good food doesn't cost the earth, environmental responsibility will play an integral role in the way we cook in the future.

Using Technology to Enhance Precision and Creativity in the Kitchen

Both professional chefs and amateur cooks have seen a sea change in their methods since technology became an integral part of the kitchen. Modern technology has revolutionized the kitchen, allowing for more efficiency and creativity with tools like smart appliances and precise culinary gear.

Imagine a professional utilizing a sous-vide equipment to get the perfect temperature every time, or a home cook using a smart oven that comes with recipe instructions already installed. Thanks to technological advancements, not only are cooking tasks made easier, but new forms of artistic expression are also made possible. Technology enhances human expertise in the future kitchen, enabling more precision, inventiveness, and culinary discovery.

Growing Interest in Health-Conscious Eating as Consumer Preferences Alter

Consumers' changing preferences will have a significant impact on the future of food preparation. An increased emphasis on mindful eating is indicative of a change in consumer needs. Diners nowadays are looking for restaurants that are socially responsible, have open sourcing policies, and serve delicious food.

Envision a menu that features plant-based options, promotes sustainable methods, and details where ingredients come from. Adapting to evolving expectations and prioritizing ethical standards in pursuit of culinary perfection is imperative for chefs and food businesses in the future, as they cater to a conscientious audience.

The Role of Culinary Schools in Cultivating Creative Thinkers

The future of food preparation is in the hands of those who will come after us in the kitchen. As a field, culinary education is transforming to provide future cooks with a well-rounded skill set that includes not just technical knowledge but also an appreciation for cultural diversity, business savvy, and sustainability.
Imagine a culinary school where students learn modern skills while experimenting with different cuisines from around the world. By

producing a new generation of chefs who are both technically adept and socially aware, culinary schools are a driving factor in the industry's upward trajectory.

Striking a Balance Between Tradition and Innovation in Gastronomy: What's Next?

Emerging gourmet trends that harmonize tradition and innovation are shaping the future of cuisine. A growing interest in genuine, impactful dining experiences is reflected in trends like traditional cooking, hyper-local sourcing, and immersive dining.

Imagine a restaurant where customers may become involved in the kitchen or learn about the history of the ingredients used to make their food. In order to provide customers with a more interactive and unforgettable experience, upcoming trends in gastronomy will place an emphasis on the whole culinary journey rather than simply the final product.

AI's Function: Redefinition of Creative Culinary Ability

One area where artificial intelligence (AI) might have a revolutionary impact is the kitchen of the future. With its ability to generate recipes and provide tailored cooking suggestions, AI is revolutionizing the culinary arts by bringing fresh perspectives, automating repetitive chores, and solving everyday problems in unique ways.

Envision an AI-powered culinary assistant that adapts to your tastes, plans meals with your nutritional needs in mind, and offers recipe suggestions based on your past cooking habits. In the future, AI will be an integral part of the kitchen, helping with tasks such as recipe creation and ensuring that people of all skill levels can enjoy a meal.

The Interdependent Link Between Members of the Community and New Food Dishes

Partnerships with locals and new ideas will be essential in the food industry of the future. Beyond the four walls of a professional kitchen, culinary innovation may be found in grassroots efforts, partnerships at the neighborhood level, and a general dedication to discovering what the culinary world has to offer.

Envision a community-run kitchen where members of the community, including farmers, chefs, and diners, work together to produce one-of-a-kind dishes. Together, innovators and the communities they serve can shape the future of cooking by strengthening bonds, establishing common ground, and envisioning a shared future for food.

Summary: A Weave of What Lies Ahead in the Food Industry

Innovation, sustainability, technological progress, and shifting culinary tastes are the threads that will weave together the future of cooking. There is a vast and varied culinary environment because the kitchen, which was previously a domain of tradition, is now a dynamic place where the past and the future meet.

Going forward, chefs will keep innovating, using technology to their advantage, and catering to the environmentally conscious tastes of their customers. With the help of community-driven initiatives, the culinary world can become more inclusive and collaborative, and a new generation of chefs may be empowered with a comprehensive understanding of their profession through culinary education.

The goals of chefs, customers, teachers, and researchers will influence the future of cooking, which is not a static concept but rather the coming together of numerous potentials. One thing is certain as we set out on our culinary adventure into uncharted territory: the kitchen, with its magical ability to bring people together, will always be a place where old and new collide, and cooking's secret mysteries are revealed in the most unexpected manner.

Tales of culinary schools, apprenticeships, and the pursuit of knowledge.

Aspiring chefs embark on their journeys in the fiery furnace of culinary discovery, where knives twirl, sauces boil, and flavors collide. In this anthology of stories, we go inside the world of culinary arts programs, apprenticeships, and the dogged quest for knowledge—a path characterized by enthusiasm, innovation, hardship, and the incredible personal growth of those brave enough to enter the demanding but ultimately rewarding field of culinary arts.

Beginning of the Culinary Journey in

Dreams of creating unforgettable meals, becoming an expert in the chemistry of flavors, and making a lasting impression on the culinary world are common starting points for many a journey. This chapter takes readers on a journey with passionate cooks as they face a maze of decisions, from choosing the best culinary school to charting a course that suits their goals in the kitchen.

Embark on a culinary education journey with Sarah, a fresh high school grad with a penchant for pastries. Is it more fitting for her aspirations to do an individualized apprenticeship with a local pastry chef, or to attend a world-renowned culinary school? She is making a choice that will shape her culinary identity and, by extension, her future, rather than merely acquiring skills.

A Web of Culinary Institutes

The culinary arts program is the furnace where unbridled enthusiasm is transformed into mastery of the craft. From elite schools with Michelin-starred chefs to community colleges that promote diversity and inclusion, this chapter delves into the varied landscapes of culinary education. As they dive headfirst into the curriculum, aspiring chefs learn techniques, develop their palate, and connect with others who share their passion for food.

Join Miguel, a student from another country who loves all kinds of food, as he explores the cultural tapestry of a world-class cooking school. By participating in both theoretical and practical training, he is able to hone his talents and gain a deeper understanding of food, culture, and the interdependence of culinary traditions.

The Crucible of Mentorship,

Apprenticeships are sacred spaces where theory and practice converge, where skilled individuals undergo a transformative process from novice to expert. Here we enter the kitchen, the furnace where master chefs teach those with aspirations of becoming cooks. Outside of the traditional classroom setting, students may immerse themselves in the sound of cooking as they listen to the clatter of pans, the sizzle of ingredients, and the wisdom that has been handed down through the years.

Embark with Maria on her culinary apprenticeship at a busy downtown restaurant. She learns the ins and outs of cooking as well as the art of timing, orchestration, and the dance that is at the center of every successful kitchen under the tutelage of a famous chef, navigating the hectic intensity of a professional kitchen.

Real-Life Stories from the Kitchen

Working long hours in a high-pressure workplace while striving for perfection is nothing new to the culinary profession. In this chapter, we are transported to the intense, pressure-filled world of professional kitchens and culinary apprenticeships, where the determination, imagination, and speed required to achieve culinary greatness are showcased in every dish.

Accompany Carlos, a young chef with big dreams of making it big in the cutthroat world of fine dining. In his dogged pursuit of culinary greatness, he faces every problem head-on, from perfecting plating techniques to achieving the perfect harmony of flavors.

In , We Discuss Culinary Individuality and New Approaches

As they learn more, all chefs develop their own distinct style—their culinary personality. The role of apprenticeships and formal culinary education in shaping students' unique culinary identities is discussed in this chapter. A chef's journey is a reflection of their character, life experiences, and goals; it may include accepting cultural influences or pushing the limits of creativity.

Ana is a cook who loves to experiment with new recipes, so step inside her world. During her time at culinary school and apprenticeships, she delves into innovative techniques, unusual ingredients, and the art of storytelling in the kitchen. Her recipes are more than simply food; they are stories that take the palate, the sense of touch, and the mind on an adventure.

International Views on the Culinary Arts

Regardless of one's location or cultural background, culinary apprenticeships and schools have become a worldwide phenomenon. In this chapter, we'll look at how chefs from all over the world add their unique blend of knowledge and experience to the culinary traditions that make up our cuisine.

Come along on a gastronomic adventure with Akiko, a chef who deftly combines the flavors of her Japanese background with those of her apprenticeship in a French culinary capital. Her culinary masterpieces serve as a proof of how varied culinary influences may live in harmony as she moves between the traditional and the modern, the global and the local.

Obstacles and Successes on the Road to Culinary Expertise

Gaining expertise in the kitchen is no picnic. In this chapter, we see the obstacles that prospective chefs encounter, such as learning complex procedures and dealing with the cutthroat restaurant industry. Success in the kitchen is a result of hard work, perseverance, and an unfaltering love for the art form.

Follow the journey of Ricardo, a chef who faced challenges but ultimately achieved his goals, as he navigates the culinary industry. His story, which begins with early failures in culinary school and ends with victories in renowned competitions, exemplifies the life-altering potential of perseverance and the drive for greatness.

Culinary Entrepreneurship: Exploring New Horizons in

No one's culinary education should be limited to the four walls of a classroom. In this chapter, we'll look at how chefs use the skills they learn in their apprenticeships and formal culinary programs to launch their own businesses. As they break new ground in the culinary industry and launch their own restaurants, these chefs are redefining what it means to be successful in the kitchen.

Take a page out of Julia's cookbook—she started a successful farm-to-table restaurant by combining her formal training with an apprenticeship program. Her journey explores the financial savvy needed to succeed in the food industry, from finding sustainable ingredients to building a signature brand.

Carrying on the Tradition and Legacy of Good Food

When cooks reach a certain point in their employment, they frequently are tasked with passing their expertise on to the following generation. In this chapter, we'll look at mentorship, culinary legacy, and the influence that seasoned chefs have on the next generation of chefs.

Take Alberto, for example. He's a seasoned chef who happily takes on the position of mentor at a cooking school. Aspiring chefs learn the ins and outs of the trade from him, but they also pick up lessons in leadership, contribution to the culinary community, and the more abstract qualities of being a chef.

In we will explore the ever-evolving culinary continuum.

There is no endpoint to the culinary journey; rather, it is a continuous process of discovering new flavors, methods, and cultural subtleties. This last section takes stock of the stories' accumulated knowledge, experiences, and variety of culinary adventures. It ponders the everlasting allure of the culinary arts and the boundless opportunities that await individuals bold enough to enter the realm of culinary academies, apprenticeships, and the dogged quest for wisdom.

Every chapter adds a distinct thread to the culinary world's rich tapestry, creating a continuum. As we conclude these tales, we acknowledge that the voyage is far from over—an adventure that goes beyond borders and time, where every chef is a storyteller, and every dish tells a story in the ongoing epic of culinary excellence.

Learning from different cultures and culinary traditions.

In the complex web of world cuisines, learning about other people's customs and recipes may be a life-altering experience that brings people together across national boundaries and languages. This deep dive examines the complexities of acquiring knowledge from other culinary traditions, revealing the significant influence it has on foodies, cooks, and the dynamic field of gastronomy as a whole.

Culinary research delves into the rich history, intricate customs, and cultural subtleties that mold a community's culinary character, going beyond just appreciating flavors and skills. The first strand of this intricate web reveals the profound relationship between food and culture. The history, geography, and traditions of a certain area are reflected in its cuisine, which in turn forms a story in and of itself.

Take the busy streets of Tokyo as an example; there, the art of sushi-making is both a culinary tradition and a reflection of Japanese aesthetics and a deep reverence for seasonal ingredients. Careful attention to detail turns raw fish and rice into a culinary masterpiece, highlighting the reciprocal relationship between culture and food. In this case, the cultural tapestry is more than just a background; it permeates the entire dining experience and shapes the foods to their core.

Crossroads where varied flavors and techniques intersect are often the result of culinary exploration that moves beyond the borders of individual civilizations. These meeting points of the culinary world serve as experimental kitchens, where new ideas are born and old boundaries of cuisine are being redrawn. Imagine the bustling food markets of Singapore, where vendors skillfully combine cuisines from Chinese, Malay, Indian, and Peranakan traditions. Reflecting the cosmopolitan character of the city-state, the strength of culinary crossroads comes from the harmonious cohabitation of many culinary traditions, not only from fusing ingredients.

Instead of limiting oneself to home cooking and chain restaurants, culinary travel opens one's mind and soul to new possibilities. Every bite becomes a narrative from a faraway place, and the plate itself becomes a passport. In this chapter, we'll take a look at how traveling the world via one's taste buds may be a life-altering experience. Immerse yourself in the delicious aromas of tagines, couscous, and fragrant spices as Maria, a gourmet connoisseur, savors Marrakech's street food. Not only does culinary tourism expose people to new cuisines, but it also gives them a glimpse into the cultural subtleties and traditions that mold a region's culinary scene.

Because of its unique capacity to bring people of different backgrounds together, food may be a potent means of promoting mutual respect and understanding. This chapter delves into the concept of culinary diplomacy, which aims to foster cross-cultural understanding, dispel misconceptions, and bring people together over a shared culinary experience. Envision a diplomatic event where the finest dishes from many countries' cuisines are prepared by a group of chefs working together. Beyond the plate, culinary diplomacy becomes a tool for promoting cultural exchange, cultivating partnerships, and encouraging discourse in our ever more interconnected globe.

Although many culinary traditions have deep historical roots, they are dynamic and change over time in response to factors such as shifting consumer preferences, new technology, and cultural dynamics. This chapter explores the ways in which time-honored culinary techniques evolve with the times, blending tradition with innovation to thrive in the dynamic world of modern cuisine.

Visit Kyoto's tea rooms to see how the centuries-old Japanese tea ceremony has been updated with technology to appeal to a modern audience. When done well, culinary traditions can serve as a link between generations, enabling people to enjoy the foods of yesteryear while also taking advantage of the opportunities presented by the modern world.

Every meal has a history, a tale that has been passed down through the years and carries the knowledge of those who came before. The significance of inherited knowledge in culinary traditions is discussed in this chapter.

Recipes that have been handed down through the years serve as living proof of the inseparable bond between generations. Come along with Roberto as he visits a small Tuscan village to see his nonna and learn the secrets of traditional pasta making. Traditional culinary knowledge is a living legacy that connects people to their ancestors via shared experiences around the table and the tastes that bring back fond memories of times spent together as a family.

Marking important dates in the calendar with special meals, festivities, and communal feasts, culinary rituals and festivals are fundamental to cultural identity. From the lavish feasts of Chinese New Year to the jubilant street food festivals of Diwali in India,

this chapter delves into the significance of culinary rituals. On the Day of the Dead, Mexico City comes alive as families assemble to make altars decorated with beloved delicacies of the deceased. Through shared customs and culinary experiences, culinary rituals bring people together, celebrating cultural history while also serving as a community statement of identity.

Some culinary traditions are in danger of becoming extinct as a result of globalization. In this chapter, we take a look at the people, places, and things that are fighting to keep the diverse tapestry of world cuisine alive and well by restoring and preserving fading culinary traditions.

We meet Amina, a Moroccan cook who is fighting to keep alive the endangered traditional Berber cuisine. Reviving and preserving culinary traditions requires more than simply writing down recipes; it also requires communities to work together.

Questions of ethics surrounding the practice of interacting with cuisines from around the world are rising to the surface as the field of culinary studies develops.

This chapter explores the ethical implications of combining aspects from other traditions into one's culinary repertoire, dives into questions of appropriation and respect, and explores the obligations that come with culinary inquiry. Think about a New York City chef who is inspired by Japanese kaiseki but struggles with the moral questions that arise when he or she uses ancient techniques without completely comprehending their cultural background. Chefs and foodies are encouraged to embrace many cultures with compassion and respect, as the ethics of culinary inquiry necessitate a nuanced approach.

When it comes to molding the worldviews of future cooks and foodies, culinary schools are indispensable. In this last section, we'll look at how culinary arts programs and schools open doors to international cuisines by teaching students about different cooking styles and the cultural factors that influence them.

Embark on a gastronomic adventure with Isabella as she learns from master chefs from all over the world at an elite international institute. Not only does a culinary education help students develop their technical abilities, but it also fosters in them a deep respect for the cultural diversity that makes up the world's cuisines.

Last but not least, a rich mosaic of human diversity is created by the weaving together of knowledge from many cultural traditions and culinary practices. Every detail in this intricate story adds to the variety and abundance of the world's cuisine.

Culinary adventurers and chefs alike take on the role of storytellers as they delve into different cultures, creating stories with every dish that honor the common bond of sharing a meal. Celebrating human diversity and acknowledging the shared joys of discovering the varied world of global cuisine, the path of learning from different cultures and culinary traditions is more than just a culinary undertaking.

Reflection on the ever-changing nature of culinary trends.

In the vibrant realm of cuisine, contemplating the ephemeral character of culinary fads reveals an enthralling story of creativity, adaptation, and the ever-shifting interaction of tastes, methods, and cultural influences. Following the ebb and flow of culinary trends, this in-depth investigation delves into what drives change, the crucial role of foodies and chefs, and the intriguing development of preferences that mold the modern culinary scene.

Changing societal dynamics, individual preferences, and culinary trends all contribute to a dynamic food industry. The forces that lead to the ever-changing nature of food trends are the starting point of this investigation. The ever-changing culinary landscape is the result of a confluence of variables, such as changes in consumer tastes, the effects of globalization, and the power of social media.

Think about how health consciousness, ethical concerns, and concerns about the environment have contributed to the recent upsurge in plant-based diets. More generally, people are rethinking the typical meat-centric plate and eating more mindfully, which is reflected in this trend. By drawing more attention to plant-based cuisine and starting a worldwide dialogue about food's future, social media platforms serve as potent catalysts.

Next, we'll look at how chefs are the ones really pushing culinary trends. In addition to being skilled cooks, chefs are also tastemakers, inventors, and trendsetters who shape public perceptions of food. The story takes place in the kitchens of trailblazers who innovate by using unusual foods, fresh methods, and fresh presentations to wow their colleagues and customers.

As part of molecular gastronomy, chefs take on the role of culinary alchemists, manipulating ingredients through a range of temperature and shape changes to produce innovative dishes. This introspective investigation continues with the trailblazing work of chefs who have made sustainability their gastronomic credo, fighting for ethical methods, using only locally produced foods, and reducing food waste.

Contemporary food is shaped by a varied tapestry of global influences, and culinary trends reflect these transitions in culture. In this investigation, we will travel through the gastronomic traditions of many cultures, the blending of different tastes, and the honoring of cultural variety via food. The story takes place in kitchens where cooks combine techniques from many cultures to make delicacies that are loved all around the world.

Imagine a restaurant where the best of both worlds collide, with a chef skillfully fusing modern French techniques with classic Japanese flavors to create a fusion that will wow even the pickiest of eaters. As a means of cultural expression, culinary trends allow chefs to honor tradition while welcoming the change that characterizes today's food scene.

The eating experience is always changing in response to new culinary trends. Immersive, multimodal encounters reimagine the conventional restaurant concept in this investigation into the world of experiential dining. This story takes place at restaurants where customers can do more than just eat; they can learn about the history of each dish, help prepare it, and develop a stronger bond with the food they eat.

Picture a restaurant where customers can watch chefs work in an open kitchen and learn about the ingredients, methods, and inspirations that go into each dish, all while enjoying delectable sensations. A yearning for a more complete involvement with the culinary arts manifests itself in the rise of experiential eating, which goes beyond mere nourishment.

The investigation veers off course when it enters the domain of reminiscence and the renaissance of vintage recipes. At a time when everyone is so focused on trying new things, foodies and chefs alike are going back to the basics to unearth the flavors, methods, and recipes that have stood the test of time. Set in modern kitchens, the story follows cooks as they give historic recipes a new spin, satisfying cravings for both tradition and creativity.

Take, for example, the recent uptick in the popularity of artisanal bread-making. In this style, bakers use traditional fermentation techniques, heirloom grains, and local influences to make bread that is both delicious and a tribute to the artistry and history of baking. In this light, culinary fads constitute a never-ending cycle in which classic ingredients and techniques influence contemporary dishes.

We go further into the phenomenon of food as cultural currency, wherein fads in the kitchen serve as symbols of societal rank, individuality, and way of life. Through the lens of how specific foods or cooking techniques become symbols of cultural capital, this story reveals the complex web of relationships between food and social dynamics, illuminating how these factors impact public opinion and personal taste.

Imagine the social status that comes with specialty coffee, where the beans used, the way they are brewed, and even the decor of coffee shops represent a certain way of life. When seen in this light, culinary trends are more than simply passing fads; they are assertions of communal and individual identities, goals, and affinities.

The influence of technology developments on gastronomic fads is examined as the story progresses. When food and technology unite, it's not just about making cooking more efficient; it's a dynamic convergence that changes the face of food as a whole. Here we go behind the scenes of modern kitchens where AI is only one of many innovative tools used by chefs to improve accuracy, imagination, and the quality of their dishes.

Picture this: at a restaurant, customers can use digital menus that take into account their likes, dislikes, dietary restrictions, and past orders to provide specific suggestions. As technology changes the way people interact with and share their culinary experiences, it also makes it easier for new culinary trends to emerge in the digital sphere.

In this version of events, culinary fads serve as messengers of international understanding and communication, extending the idea of cuisine as a diplomatic tool. In this investigation, the ability of food to bridge cultural divides, promote mutual understanding, and act as a form of "soft diplomacy" is uncovered. Imagine festivals that bring together cooks from all over the world to discuss their recipes and traditions, fostering a sense of mutual understanding via food.

Take sushi, for example, which has gone well beyond its Japanese roots to become a cherished and ubiquitous cuisine all around the world. Think about the impact that this has had. As such, culinary trends serve as cultural ambassadors, helping individuals from all walks of life to bond over a common language: food.

The investigation continues by delving into the complexities of sustainability as a motivating factor in modern food trends. Environmental awareness is on the rise, and with it, a movement towards greener and more ethical cooking methods among both chefs and foodies. Scenes set in kitchens where chefs promote sustainable seafood options, use zero-waste methods, and put an emphasis on seasonal, locally produced ingredients.

Picture a restaurant menu that doesn't just list the ingredients and their origins, but also stresses the significance of buying from local farmers and reducing waste. In the context of sustainability, culinary trends mirror a larger social movement towards conscientious consumerism and a dedication to caring for the environment.

The investigation continues to go off course, touching on wellness and the meeting point of trendy diets and health-conscious ways of living. Culinary trends are showing a move towards plant-centric, nutrient-dense foods as people become more aware of the connection between diet and health. As the story develops, we see chefs tinkering with superfoods, making drinks with hidden functions, and planning menus that put an emphasis on taste and health.

As people look for both gastronomic enjoyment and overall health, adapt genic components have been making an appearance in all sorts of drinks and smoothie bowls. The way people approach food and culinary enjoyment is influenced by current culinary trends, which in the context of wellness represent the mutually beneficial relationship between food and health.

Reflecting on what the future holds for culinary trends is where the exploration comes to a close. Given the dynamic nature of the food industry, what does the future hold? Finally, this section makes some educated guesses about future developments, possible paradigm shifts, and the ever-changing tastes in food. Climate change, technology advancement, and cultural interaction are some of the variables that the story mulls over as they relate to the future of food and the ways it will be prepared and enjoyed.

Envision a world where chefs use data-driven insights to personalize diners' experiences, discover uncharted territories in fermentation, and tap into the power of alternative proteins. In this other reality, culinary trends form a kaleidoscope landscape where new ideas and time-honored techniques blend, and the dynamic nature of the culinary arts enchants diners around the world.

Reflection on the ephemeral nature of food trends, in the end, shows a complex and dynamic story. Society, culture, technology, and the collective imagination of foodies and chefs all have a role in shaping culinary trends, which are more than just fads in taste. As we explore this diverse tapestry, we discover that the culinary scene is a platform where new ideas and long-standing practices meet, where tastes can tell stories, and where the dynamic nature of gastronomy influences our enjoyment of food.

Anticipation of what the future holds for food and cooking

In the vast world of gastronomy, wondering what the future of food and cooking brings is an exciting adventure into the unknown, where innovations in the kitchen, sustainability, and the changing dynamics of the world's taste are all up for grabs. This in-depth investigation sets out on an exploratory mission, exploring the hypothetical terrain of new trends, game-changing technology, and the far-reaching effects of social, environmental, and cultural changes on the future of food production, preparation, and consumption.

The story develops as we learn about the revolutionary possibilities of different proteins. The hope for a future where proteins originating from plants, cell cultures, or insects take center stage is growing in tandem with the worldwide desire for sustainable food supplies. Let your mind wander to a future where plant-based burgers are the norm rather than the exception, appealing to a conscientious and health-conscious clientele.

In this other future, chefs are free to explore a wide range of plant proteins, from seitan and tempeh to novel dishes made from algae and fungus, pushing the bounds of traditional taste and texture. Everyone from vegetarians and vegans to those in the mainstream of the food industry is waiting for a protein revolution that will change the way we think about what a healthy, filling meal should be.

The adventure continues by delving into precision agriculture and its game-changing possibilities in the food supply chain. One vision for a more sustainable and resilient food system is the integration of smart agriculture technology, hydroponics, and vertical farming into the culinary scene in the not-too-distant future. Envision cityscapes dotted with vertical farms, continuously harvesting a wealth of seasonal, locally grown food.

Regardless of location or weather, chefs in this future have access to a wide variety of fresh produce, putting the conventional idea of seasonal availability in the background. Harvesting ingredients at their height of maturity reduces waste and carbon footprints associated with standard agriculture operations, making the anticipation of a hyper-local and hyper-fresh gourmet experience a reality.

After that, we'll look at how technology interacts with the culinary arts. We look forward to a future where robotics, augmented reality, and artificial intelligence are seamlessly integrated into cooking areas. It will open up new frontiers of accessibility, efficiency, and creativity. Envision a kitchen where algorithms powered by artificial intelligence assess taste profiles, provide individualized recipe suggestions according to tastes and dietary limitations, and even lend a hand when cooking.

In this hypothetical future, smart kitchen tools make even the most complex recipes easy to follow, making cooking a more accessible and inclusive activity for all. We are about to witness a sea change in our relationship with the culinary arts as we prepare for a future where technology improves the efficiency and creativity of chefs.

The story progresses with an investigation into the confluence of the culinary arts with health, looking forward to a time when the idea of food as medicine is more deeply embedded in our culinary awareness. Here in the future, we dream of a culinary scene where dietitians and health experts work together to craft dishes that are a feast for the senses and good for you.

Envision a restaurant where dishes are chosen for their flavor as well as their potential to promote health via the use of functional ingredients. One day, the culinary arts will change the way people think about and interact with the food they eat by playing an active role in preventive healthcare, resolving nutritional deficiencies, and encouraging holistic well-being.

Next, we'll take a look at personalized nutrition, a rapidly developing field that aims to one day use data analytics, biometrics, and genetics to provide nutritional recommendations based on each person's unique health profile and genetic composition. The hope is that in the not-too-distant future, restaurants will have menus that change on the fly to accommodate customers' individual dietary restrictions and tastes.

Imagine a future where people may improve their health, energy levels, and vitality with individualized meal planning, made possible by genetic insights. We are about to undergo a sea change in our relationship with food and cooking as we prepare for a future where personalized dietary needs are more important than a cookie-cutter approach to nutrition.

Next, we enter the sustainable realm, where we look forward to a future when regenerative agriculture, circular food systems, and a dedication to minimizing food waste are front and center. Envision a restaurant scene where regenerative methods are standard operating procedure and where farms have an emphasis on soil preservation, biodiversity, and carbon sequestration when procuring ingredients.

We hope that in the not-too-distant future, sustainable practices like composting, zero-waste cooking, and ethical ingredient sourcing will become standard fare in the culinary world. Imagine a restaurant that follows a continuous cycle of food production, starting from the farm and ending with the soil. A greater understanding of the interdependence between food, the environment, and human health has led many to dream of a day when sustainability is intrinsic to the story of food.

The investigation veers off course as it enters the realm of culinary innovation, looking forward to a day when culinary frontiers are pushed to their limits. In this hypothetical future, the idea of a meal is upended by a culinary scene that features experimental flavors, textures, and presentations. Imagine a dessert made not with conventional ingredients but with 3D-printed sweets that play with your sense of texture and sweetness.

Hopes for a world where molecular gastronomy, fermentation, and culinary alchemy give birth to new types of food are fueling the culinary revolution. Armed with a toolbox of cutting-edge methods and unusual ingredients, chefs take on the role of culinary avant-garde artists, challenging the norms and expectations of what is considered edible and acceptable.

After that, the story shifts to focus on the hope for a future when cuisine is more diverse and welcoming. In this hypothetical future, the food industry is more diverse in terms of representation and the flavors it offers, and the world of cuisine is more diverse in terms of the people that make up the industry. Envision a world where chefs of all colors, nationalities, and cultures are not outliers but rather essential cogs in the wheel of international cuisine.

Imagine a restaurant where the menu showcases a diverse array of international influences, where flavors from all over the world come together to create a dining experience that is both harmonious and inclusive. There will be a change towards a more equal and richer culinary world when the culinary arts proactively break down boundaries, challenge preconceptions, and offer a platform for cross-cultural understanding and enjoyment.

Towards the end of the story, the reader would have eagerly anticipated a completely new way to eat. A more fluid and individualized gastronomic experience is anticipated in this future scenario as the lines between home cooking and restaurant eating blur. Think of a future when people can easily make restaurant-quality food in the comfort of their own homes using state-of-the-art culinary technologies.

Beyond the four walls of a typical restaurant, many dream of a future where eating is an immersive, multimodal experience. Envision a world where virtual reality enhances the dining experience, taking guests on a journey through various culinary locales with each course and its carefully designed visual and audio story. We are looking forward to a future where the art of dining is combined with the ingenuity of designers, architects, and engineers. This will completely change the way we enjoy food.

The educational community looks forward to a day when culinary arts programs and schools adapt to the ever-changing demands of the industry. The hope for the future is that schools will teach students more than just how to cook; they will also teach them about nutrition, cultural aspects of food, and the importance of preserving natural resources.

Envision a culinary academy that teaches students not only how to cook, but also how to source materials ethically, how to use science to their advantage, and the cultural importance of different cuisines. A paradigm shift is needed in the way we train the chefs of the future if we want culinary schools to be agents of revolutionary change, creating cooks who aren't merely competent in their craft but also knowledgeable about it and eager to make an impact.

The story continues with the hope of a more united international foodie community. The ideal future for the food industry is one in which producers, chefs, and fans work together across national boundaries to exchange ideas, recipes, and techniques in a truly global culinary innovation exchange. Imagine a world where cooks from other continents can connect in real-time through digital platforms, creating a cross-cultural discussion that doesn't care about geography.

A significant shift in our perspective and interaction with food is anticipated in the future when the culinary arts serve as a means of fostering worldwide understanding, admiration, and cooperation. A common legacy that brings people together from all over the globe, the variety and abundance of international cuisines serve as more than simply an inspiration as the culinary communities grow increasingly interdependent.

As the story nears its conclusion, its focus shifts to the hope of approaching food and cooking with greater awareness and mindfulness. Imagine a world where people in the food industry, from consumers to chefs, take into account the social, environmental, and ethical consequences of their decisions. Envision a society where customers are more than simply buyers; they are active members of a food system that prioritizes openness, accountability, and camaraderie.

A greater understanding of the relationship between our dietary habits and the health of our planet and its people has led many to dream of a future where food plays a more active role in promoting positive change rather than merely being a commodity. People look forward to a future where the tales, values, and ideals included in the food they eat are as important as the tastes themselves, as the culinary scene evolves.

Finally, looking forward to the culinary and culinary-related adventures that lie ahead is an exciting adventure full of endless possibilities. Innovation, awareness, and global collaboration are the threads that will weave the future of food into a tapestry that includes the transformative potential of alternative proteins, the integration of technology into culinary spaces, a redefined approach to health and sustainability, and the celebration of cultural diversity.

As we look forward to this future, we are at the dawn of a culinary renaissance, a period when the culinary scene is about to undergo a dramatic shift. The path ahead invites us to do more than just guess; it compels us to actively mold and take part in the story of the culinary arts as it unfolds. As individuals and as a community, we have the ability to shape a future where food serves as more than just fuel; it can also be a medium for expression, building relationships, and positive transformation. The future of food and cooking should reflect our hopes for a more sustainable, inclusive, and nourishing globa culinary tapestry, and looking forward isn't merely about wondering what's to come; it's also about actively co-creating that future.

Reflection on the transformative power of cooking and the shared human experience in the kitchen.

In the middle of every kitchen, amidst the clang of cookware, the steady chop of veggies, and the cacophony of sizzling ingredients, is a magic that goes beyond just making food. In this in-depth analysis, we look into the universal human experience of being in the kitchen and the life-altering potential of food preparation. Beyond the recipes and cooking methods, it delves into the core of cooking and the joy of sharing one's creations with others.

The Crucible of the Kitchen: An Introduction
A lot of life changes take place in the kitchen, which is why it's called the "heart" of the house. Here, uncooked materials are transformed into something delicious, pleasurable, and culturally significant. The act of cooking itself is a unifying force, bringing people together from all walks of life and sharing a common bond via the commonality of the human experience. This contemplation delves into the culinary crucible, investigating the life-altering potential of food preparation and the deep bonds formed amongst cooks and their guests.

Before We Get to the Ingredients,Mastering the Art of Cooking
A meal is more than just the result of a sequence of operations in the kitchen. Beyond the material changes taking place in the oven or pot, there is an alchemical process at work.

This chapter explores the magic of cooking by looking at how mixing ingredients is a metaphor for how different parts of life come together. As the bread rises in the oven and the onions sizzle in a pan, each stage of preparation reflects a personal or communal transformation.

A Cultural Tapestry in the Common Kitchen

In the kitchen, people from all walks of life come together to share food, customs, and language. In this chapter, we look at how cooking together as a human society weaves together different cultures to form a mosaic that mirrors the rich diversity of our world. The act of cooking serves as a bridge across generations, continents, and traditions; via anthologies and shared recipes, we trace the connections that bind kitchens across the globe.

A Spiritual and Physical Diet through the Ritual of Cooking

In addition to its functional purposes, cooking frequently assumes a ritualistic character, as it nourishes both the body and the spirit. The symbolic and sacred aspects of cooking are explored in this chapter, looking at how kitchen rituals can bring solace, community, and enlightenment. Cooking as a ritual weaves a story that extends beyond the plate, from the creation of exceptional meals for special occasions to the everyday rituals that mark the passing of time.

Life and Legacy Lessons Learned in the Kitchen

The kitchen becomes a classroom when people join together to cook, and the lessons taught there go well beyond the realm of food. Lessons like perseverance, creativity, collaboration, and patience can be learned via the simple act of cooking, as discussed in this chapter. With the help of personal stories and introspection, we can piece together the knowledge that has been handed down through the years, illuminating the kitchen as a place where people may learn to cook and also get perspective on the bigger picture of life.

Working Together in the Kitchen: Mastering the Art of Cooking

In the kitchen, people of many walks of life often work together to make a meal that is more delicious and more satisfying than the sum of its components. In this chapter, we'll take a look at the finer points of cooking as a group, discussing how sharing a meal together can bring people closer, build stronger bonds, and make memories that last a lifetime. We explore the many settings where people get together to cook, from shared kitchens to group cooking lessons, to discover how the common bond of food brings people together.

The Healing Kitchen—Feeding More Than Just the Body

There is a therapeutic aspect to cooking that goes beyond just the flavor. This chapter explores the therapeutic potential of the kitchen by looking at how making and sharing food can alleviate stress and improve mental health. Whether it's the comforting embrace of home-cooked soup or the shared experience of making meals for a friend who is grieving, the kitchen is a place where the transformational power of food reaches into the spiritual and emotional aspects of human life.

A Flavor of Nostalgia through Food and Memories

Some foods have a way of bringing people back in time, to particular experiences. Discover how the smells, flavors, and textures of particular dishes may evoke strong feelings of nostalgia as this chapter delves into the link between cooking and memory. The kitchen serves as a gateway to reminiscence, allowing us to relish not just the tastes but also the sentiments and tales associated with our beloved dishes, whether they are traditional family recipes or beloved dishes from our childhood.

The International Link in Food and Drink

As a global community, we can all relate to the universality of the kitchen experience. In this chapter, we explore how kitchens around the world have become epicurean meeting places due to travel, technology, and the sharing of culinary ideas. By looking at social media, cooking shows, and international culinary collaborations, we can see how people from other continents may share and celebrate their love of food through the culinary connection, which goes beyond geographical boundaries.

The Development of Flavor—From Custom to New Approaches

A dynamic palette that swings between tradition and innovation characterizes the common human experience in the kitchen. This chapter follows the development of flavor by looking at how different cuisines have managed to keep their traditions alive while also incorporating new ideas and techniques. The kitchen is an ever-changing arena where innovative techniques and fusion cuisines push the limits of taste, mirroring the human capacity for adaptation and inventiveness in the kitchen.

Visions for a Revolutionary Kitchen of the Future

This last chapter looks ahead while we consider the future in light of the transformational potential of food and the commonality of the human experience in the kitchen. How will the food industry evolve in the future?

What impact will environmental concerns, cultural changes, and technology breakthroughs have on tomorrow's kitchens? Wondering what the future holds, we delve into imaginative stories and forward-thinking ideas, looking forward to the kitchen's role as a catalyst for change and community in the dynamic fabric of human history.

Final Thoughts: A Common Gastronomic Journey

Finally, when we consider how cooking may change our lives and how we all spend time in the kitchen together, we find a complex web of history, culture, memory, and new ideas.

Through its alchemical transformation, the kitchen goes beyond its practical role and becomes a haven where people can find sustenance for their physical, emotional, and spiritual selves as well as for their community as a whole. Cooking becomes more than just a daily task when we immerse ourselves in the tales, rituals, and teamwork that surround it. It becomes a shared culinary adventure that unites us via the common language of food and the deep human experience it encompasses.

9 789358 683387

Printed at Repro India Ltd.